Grace vs. Judgment: Which One Is It?

By Keith A. Butler

Harrison House
Tulsa, OK

All Scripture quotations are taken from the *King James Version* of the Bible.

18 17 16 15   10 9 8 7 6 5 4 3

Grace vs. Judgment: Which One Is It?
ISBN 13: 978-160683-983-6
Copyright © 2014 by Keith A. Butler

Published by Harrison House Publishers
Tulsa, OK 74145
www.harrisonhouse.com

Printed in the United States of America. All rights reserved under International Copyright Law. Contents and/or cover may not be reproduced in whole or in part in any form without the express written consent of the Publisher.

Table of Contents

Exploring Scripture that answers the question of whether great grace and judgment can be operative at the same time in the life of believers on earth

INTRODUCTION

A controversy over the issue of grace vs. judgment is sweeping across the church of the Lord Jesus Christ, both in the United States and overseas. I have been a licensed and ordained minister in the pulpit for forty years, so I have seen these extreme trends take hold, go away, and then come back again. Satan plays the same tricks on every generation.

The church has a tendency to fall into the ditch on either side of the road, yet the truth is usually found somewhere in the middle. My wife, Pastor Deborah, was raised in a church that focused on judgment. After I was born again, I also attended a church where the messages all revolved around the topic of fire from heaven, brimstone, and damnation. The minister of the church used to tell me that I would go to hell for playing checkers! And I saw the same people get saved every week, because they were afraid that fire would fall from heaven.

When we moved to attend Bible school, we were introduced to grace churches. These churches focused on another extreme position. They believed that if you were saved, it didn't matter how you lived or what you did—you could kill, rape, lie, steal, or whatever—because the grace of God covered all sins. They believed there were no consequences for their actions. Some even went so far as to say that you didn't have to confess sin, because there's not a hell, and if there was one, God wouldn't allow anyone to go there anyway.

In short, the extreme judgment churches say that we are all unworthy and unrighteous. The extreme grace churches say that there can be no judgment for the believer. Which one is it—grace or judgment? In this book, we will explore what the Word says about this topic, so you will know how to respond when you encounter these polarized positions. We will look at this issue in the context of all Scripture, so you will clearly see God's plan for grace and judgment.

I was teaching on this topic at a ministers' conference not too long ago in Italy. They had recently split over the issue of grace. Many of the evangelical pastors in the country were there and after I taught on this subject, they asked, "Will you please come back?" They were set free! Wrong teaching brings bondage, but right teaching brings liberty and freedom! It is my prayer that the truth of God's Word in the pages of this book will also bring you liberty and freedom.

Chapter One

A Scriptural Tour of Grace

What do the Scriptures say about the grace issue? In order to determine this, we need to do three things. First, we must identify the audience to whom a specific passage is addressed. For instance, in 1 Corinthians 10:32, the Apostle Paul says: *"Give none offence, neither to the Jews, nor to the Gentiles, nor to the church of God."* We are each a member of at least one of these three people groups on the earth—Jew, Gentile, or the church of the living God. In order to understand Scripture, we first need to know which group is being addressed in that particular verse.

If Paul is talking to the Gentiles and we try to apply it to the Jews, then we will get the wrong interpretation. On the other hand, if Paul is talking to the Jews and we try to apply it to the church of God, we will also get the wrong interpretation. So we need to ask ourselves this question: "Who is he talking to, and does this apply to us or to someone else?" Much of Paul's writings on the subject of grace are written to Jews about the differences between law and grace. Everywhere Paul went, Jews confronted him. Since Paul first went to the synagogue when he came into a new town, he would tell them about the message of salvation. Some people would believe and receive Jesus as Lord, yet they would still continue to follow all of the machinations of the law by offering sacrifices, wearing certain clothing, and keeping certain days.

Second, we must read each verse in context, familiarizing ourselves with the truths in Scripture that precede and follow the word or passage, thus gaining understanding and insight that will be invaluable in determining the meaning.

Third, we must define the terms. If we have a different definition for the word being used than the speaker has, there will be confusion. It's the same when we have a conversation with someone. We need to make sure that both parties are using that word in the same way—same definition and application. If not, then there will be confusion and conflicts. For instance, my wife comes from a family of nine boys and three girls. Her experience of dinner and my experience of dinner are totally different. Her mother cooked with commercial cookware in order to hold all the food she needed to make for a family of their size. She would place a kettle piled high with spaghetti on the table, along with a stack of paper plates and Styrofoam cups filled with Kool-Aid. Then they would pray, and it was every person for himself.

In my home, however, dinner was very traditional. I come from a family of three children, so my mother prepared a full meal and used formal place settings. Our meals consisted of meat, starches, vegetables, and dessert. My experience of dinner and my understanding of the word "dinner" were not better than my wife's; they were just different. So when Deborah and I first got married and I came home for dinner, I expected to have the same experience I had at my mother's house. The first time I came home from work, Deborah had spaghetti, paper plates, and Styrofoam cups with Kool-Aid on the table. I said, "What is this?"

She said, "What? This is dinner!"

Needless to say, we had our first conflict over the issue of dinner. And it was all because we had different definitions for the word "dinner." So as you can see, incompatible definitions can cause trouble!

Defining Judgment and Grace

While doing a study in the New Testament, I found seventeen definitions for the words "judge" and "judgment" and eighteen definitions for the word "grace". If we use the wrong definition for these words, we will not rightly divide the Word, and we will be in jeopardy of arriving at a doctrine that is not scriptural.

The New Testament is translated from the Greek, so we need to look at the original Greek language to determine what the writers meant. The Greek word for "judgment" is *krima*, which means a verdict or a lawsuit; and the word for "judge" is *krino*, which means to decide mentally or judicially; try, condemn, punish, avenge, conclude, damn, decree, determine, esteem, ordain, call into question, sentence to, or think. Some of the more negative meanings come immediately to our minds when we hear the word "judge" but notice that "to judge" can also mean "to esteem, determine, or think about." In other words, this word can be either positive or negative, depending upon how it is used.

The Greek word for "grace" is *charis*, which means graciousness, acceptable, benefit, favor, gift, joy, liberality, pleasure, assistance from God, and the anointing or power. It can also mean the manifested measure of the Holy Spirit which brings about the fruit and gifts of the Spirit, the results of the Holy Spirit, and the work of God. At times, it is translated as thankworthy, thanksgiving, or thankfulness. Grace is also the name of the Holy Spirit.

Let me address one more area where people mix up words and become confused. Many people use the terms *grace, mercy,* and *righteousness* interchangeably, but these are three different Greek words that have three different meanings. The word "mercy" in the Greek is *eleos,* which means to be compassionate in word or deed. *Webster's Dictionary* says that the word "compassionate" means having a disposition that is inclined to be easily moved by the distress, sufferings, wants and infirmities of others. In other words, it means having a heart that is tender. For example, in Matthew 14:14, we read that even though Jesus had just found out about the beheading of John the Baptist—one of the people closest to Him—and had departed by ship to a desert place—He still had compassion, or mercy, on the people who followed Him and healed their sick.

We only have to read Hebrews 4:16, to discover that grace and mercy have different definitions. *"Let us therefore come boldly unto the throne of grace, that we may obtain mercy, and find grace to help in time of need."* In this context, grace is referring to assistance when we need it. We can find both compassion and help at the throne!

People often confuse grace with righteousness. The word "righteousness" in the Greek is *dikaiosuné*, which means justification or right standing with God. Righteousness is about our place in Christ. When we talk about not having a sin consciousness, we're talking about what happened to us regarding our position in Christ. That is not the definition of grace.

A Scriptural Tour of Grace

Let's go through Scripture and take a look at the word "grace" in context, in order to determine its meaning and see how its meaning can differ. In other words, we first find the word and look at it in context, then we fit our lives and teaching to the meaning of that word.

- *"And when the chief Shepherd shall appear, ye shall receive a crown of glory that fadeth not away. Likewise, ye younger, submit yourselves unto the elder. Yea, all of you be subject one to another, and be clothed with humility: for God resisteth the proud, and **giveth grace to the humble"** (1 Peter 5:4-5, emphasis mine).* The word "grace" in this context means assistance. He gives assistance to the humble.

- Let's look at this same meaning in another context, James 4:6: **"But he giveth more grace. *Wherefore he saith, God resisteth the proud, but giveth grace unto the humble"*** *(emphasis mine)*. God gives the help of the Holy Spirit to those who will bow down and say, "I don't have the power,

11

so I'm not going to lean on my power, Lord. Like Paul, I'm going to lean on Yours."

- *"Of how much sorer punishment, suppose ye, shall he be thought worthy, who have trodden under foot the Son of God, and hath counted the blood of the covenant, wherewith he was sanctified, an unholy thing, and hath done despite unto the* **Spirit of grace**" (*Hebrews 10:29, emphasis mine*). The spirit of grace is one of the names of the Holy Spirit.

- *"For if I by grace be a partaker, why am I evil spoken of for that for which I give thanks"* (*1 Corinthians 10:30, emphasis mine*). Paul is talking about whether or not people can eat food dedicated to idols. The word "grace" in this context means thanksgiving.

- *"Let your speech be always with grace, seasoned with salt, that ye may know how ye ought to answer every man"* (*Colossians 4:6, emphasis mine*). The word "salt" in the Greek is defined as prudence, and the word "grace" is defined as graciousness and acceptable. In other words, we must let our speech always be acceptable and prudent.

- *"Therefore, as ye abound in every thing, in faith, and utterance, and knowledge and in all diligence, and in your love to us, see that ye abound in this grace also"* (*2 Corinthians 8:7, emphasis mine*). Go back to the beginning of that chapter to determine the meaning of the word "grace". "*Moreover, brethren, we do you to wit of* **the grace of God bestowed** *on the churches of Macedonia, how that in a great trial of affliction* *the abundance of their joy and their deep poverty abounded unto the riches of their liberality" (vv. 1-2, emphasis mine).* Paul is talking about their giving. *"For to their power, I bear record, yea, and beyond their power they were willing of themselves; Praying us with much intreaty that we* **would receive the gift**, *and take upon us the fellowship* [partnership] *of the ministering to the saints" (vv. 3-4, emphasis mine).* Some translations use the word "grace" for "gift": that we would **receive the grace**.

This discourse about the grace of giving continues in Second Corinthians 9, where Paul says:

- *"But this I say, He which soweth sparingly shall reap also sparingly; and he which soweth bountifully shall reap also bountifully. Every man according as he purposeth in his heart, so let him give; not grudgingly, or of necessity: for God loveth a cheerful giver.* ***And God is able to make all grace abound toward you****; that ye, always having all sufficiency in all things, may abound to every good work"* (vv. 6-8, emphasis mine). Paul is not talking about our standing in Christ; he's not talking about whether we confess our sins or not. He is saying that those who give a lot, receive a lot—and those who don't give much, receive little.

- *"Likewise, ye husbands, dwell with them according to knowledge, giving honour unto the wife, as unto the weaker vessel, and as being **heirs together of the grace of life**; that* *your prayers be not hindered"* (1 Peter 3:7, emphasis mine). The word "grace" used here means benefit. In other words, a man should not fall out with his wife. The couple should stay in love and operate in unity, so they both can benefit in life.

- *"Receiving the end of your faith, even the salvation of your souls. Of which salvation the prophets have enquired and searched diligently, **who prophesied of the grace that should come unto you**"* (1 Peter 1:9-10, emphasis mine). In this context, the word "grace" means graciousness. I will discuss this word in more detail later.

Let's continue to walk through the Bible and look at the word "grace" in context.

- **"By whom we have received grace** *and apostleship, for obedience to the faith among all nations, for his name"* (Romans 1:5, emphasis mine). The grace is the anointing! Paul received the anointing, or the power of God, to stand in the office of the apostle. He had grace on him to do the job to which he had been called. I have grace on me to do what God has called me to do. And so do you!

- *"And the Word was made flesh, and dwelt among us, (and we beheld his glory, the glory as of the only begotten of the Father,) **full of grace and truth**"* (John 1:14, emphasis mine). The word "full" is the word *plérés*, a word which means to be covered over. Jesus was full of the grace of God. Jesus was covered over with the grace of God. Jesus was also full of truth, and He defined truth in John 17:17, *"Thy word is truth."*

- Since Jesus was covered over with grace, what was the nature of that grace? Acts 10:38 says, *"How God anointed Jesus of Nazareth with the Holy Ghost and with power: who went about doing good, and healing all that were oppressed of the devil; for God was with him."* God, the Father, anointed Jesus with the Holy Ghost and with power. The word "anointed" means to pour upon or cover over. Thus, in this context, grace refers to the anointing. Jesus was covered with the anointing.

- In Second Corinthians 12, we read that Paul had a demon spirit buffeting him. *"For this thing I besought the Lord thrice, that it might depart from me. And he said unto me, **My grace is sufficient for thee**: for my strength is made perfect in weakness"* (*v. 8-9, emphasis mine*).

- Paul calls the grace of God his strength. The word "strength" is *dunamis*, the word from which we derive the term dynamite. It means inherent supernatural, miraculous power. In this context, the grace of God is the power of Christ.

- In other words, God says, "My power is sufficient for you. My strength or my power is made complete or perfect in your weakness." Paul received this revelation, saying, *"Most gladly therefore will I rather glory in my infirmities, that the power of Christ may rest upon me"* (*v. 9*).

Let's look at another use of the word *grace* by Paul.

*   *"For this cause I Paul, the prisoner of Jesus Christ for you Gentiles, If ye have heard of the* **dispensation of the grace of God** *which is given me to you-ward.... Whereof I was made a minister,* **according to the gift of the grace of God given unto me** *by the effectual working of his power"* (*Ephesians 3:1, 2, 7, emphasis mine*). Paul is talking about the anointing. He's talking about the manifested measure of the Holy Spirit which brings about the gifts of God.

Are you starting to see that there are many definitions for grace in Scripture? Can you see that if we use the wrong definition, we will misunderstand the truth?

Chapter Two

Great Grace, Great Judgment

Now that we have an understanding of some of the definitions of the word "grace" and know what this term means in context, let's take a look at something else that will help us grasp a better revelation of grace and judgment. Let's find the answer to the question: **Can Christians experience judgment, or do we live in an age of grace where there is no judgment on earth for a believer?**

First, let's take a look at Acts 11:22-23

Then tidings of these things came unto the ears of the church which was in Jerusalem: and they sent forth Barnabas, that he should go as far as Antioch. Who, when he came, and had seen the grace of God, was glad, and exhorted them all, that with purpose of heart they would cleave unto the Lord.

Barnabas saw the grace of God. He didn't see a place of right standing; he saw the results or the work of God on the Gentiles. He came to certain conclusions and drew up his report about them. For some background, turn to Acts Chapter 4. The Sanhedrin council had called the disciples on the carpet for preaching about Jesus and healing in His name, saying, "You can't preach or teach anymore in this name, and if you do, we're going to kill you."

> *And being let go, they went to their own company, and reported all that the chief priests and elders had said unto them. And when they heard that, they lifted up their voice to God with one accord, and said, Lord, thou art God, which hast made heaven, and earth, and the sea, and all that in them is (Acts 4:23-24).*

Remember, three thousand people were saved on the first day. *"And the Lord added to the church daily such as should be saved"* (*Acts 2:47*). There were at least 3,000 people praying the same thing at the same time—the second Psalm.

> *And now, Lord, behold their threatenings: and grant unto thy servants, that with all boldness they may speak thy word, by stretching forth thine hand to heal; and that signs and wonders may be done by the name of thy holy child Jesus. And when they had prayed, the place was shaken where they were assembled together; and they were all filled with the Holy Ghost, and they spake the word of God with boldness. And the multitude of them that believed were of one heart and of one soul: neither said any of them that ought of the things which he possessed was his own; but they had all things common. And with great power gave the apostles witness of the resurrection*

*of the Lord Jesus: and **great grace** was upon them all (Acts 4:29-33, emphasis mine).*

The Great Grace of Giving

Scripture doesn't say that the people gave *some* of what they had; it says they gave *all* that they had. This is an amazing work of grace. *For people to give all that they have is a work of the Holy Spirit.* Some people may be a big giver to one ministry or another, but I don't think there's any partner who would meet this criteria. To do so, not only would they have to empty out all of their bank account, but they would also have to give away their clothes, their car, their condo, house or apartment, and all of their possessions.

The Holy Spirit got involved in this work of great grace! It was exceeding grace—a magnitude of grace—that caused them to give all they had and distribute it so everybody had everything they needed.

Neither was there any among them that lacked: for as many as were possessors of lands or houses sold them, and brought the prices of the things that were sold, And laid them down at the apostles' feet: and distribution was made unto every man according as he had need. And Joses, who by the apostles was surnamed Barnabas, (which is, being interpreted, the son of consolation,) a Levite, and of the country of Cyprus, having land, sold it, and brought the money, and laid it at the apostles' feet.

> *But a certain man named Ananias, with Sapphira his wife,*
> *sold a possession, and kept back part of the price, his wife also*
> *being privy to it, and brought a certain part, and laid it at the*
> *apostles' feet (Acts 4:34–5:2).*

Ananias and Sapphira were part of the multitude in the church that was involved in praying and having all things in common. They were new believers.

> *But Peter said, Ananias, why hath Satan filled thine heart to*
> *lie to the Holy Ghost, and to keep back part of the price of the*
> *land? Whiles it remained, was it not thine own? and after*
> *it was sold, was it not in thine own power? why hast thou*
> *conceived this thing in thine heart? thou hast not lied unto*
> *men, but unto God (vv. 3–4).*

Ananias only laid down, at Peter's feet, some of the money he got for his land. He pretended to give it all, but he didn't. He kept the rest. The problem wasn't that he didn't give all the money. He had the right to not sell any of the land, to sell the land and keep half of it for himself, or to make any other arrangement. The issue was that he lied to the Holy Ghost. He lied to the One who was the grace of God.

This was a time of great grace, a time of the full operation of the Spirit. The power was turned up! What happened?

> *And Ananias hearing these words fell down, and gave up the*
> *ghost: and great fear came on all them that heard these things*
> *(v. 5).*

In other words, Ananias fell down dead and the young men went out and buried him. That is judgment! But why was judgment so severe here? Most of us have told a lie at some point in our lives, yet we didn't fall over dead, so why did Ananias and Sapphira die? During the time of great grace—great manifestation—the power is turned up! That's a wonderful benefit, but always remember that unto whom much is given, much is required (see Luke 12:48).

Turned-Up Power

Jesus could be trusted by the Father so He had the Spirit without measure. Jesus said, "I can't do anything without God. I don't do anything without God. I don't even say anything except what He tells me to say." The power on Jesus could be turned up all the way, but the power isn't turned up all the way with us. If we had the power turned up all the way, it would be disastrous for us and others, just like it was for Ananias and Sapphira. If God ever says that anything is damned, it is damned forever. He isn't fast and loose with His words, and Jesus wasn't either—so neither should we be.

Shortly after Anaias died and was buried, his wife came in. She didn't know anything about what had happened to Anaias.

And it was about the space of three hours after, when his wife, not knowing what was done, came in. And Peter answered unto her, Tell me whether ye sold the land for so much? And she said, Yea, for so much. Then Peter said unto her, How is it that ye have agreed together to tempt the Spirit of the Lord? behold, the feet of them which have buried thy husband are at the door, and shall carry thee out. Then fell she down straightway at his feet, and yielded up the ghost: and the young men came in, and found her dead, and, carrying her forth, buried her by her husband (vv. 7-10).

Wait a minute! Notice that the people were so moved by the Holy Spirit that they were taking their property and their land—everything—and giving the proceeds to people whom they've never met. Yet, at the same time, two fellow believers die on the spot. How could this happen?

And great fear came upon all the church, and upon as many as heard these things. And by the hands of the apostles were many signs and wonders wrought among the people (vv. 11-12).

Let's take a look at the following comments:

- And great grace—a large measure of the inward power of the Holy Ghost was upon them all, directing all their thoughts, words and actions. (*Explanatory Notes on the Whole Bible,* John Wesley, 1754-65).

- Great grace, much favor and assistance from God were granted them. (*Family Bible: The New Testament of our Lord and Saviour Jesus Christ,* by Justin Edwards, 1851, p. 185).

- God answered their prayer and blessed them with a great measure of the Holy Ghost which brought upon the gracious fruit of the Spirit. (*The Brethren New Testament Commentary*)[1]

The fruit of the Spirit, specifically the first fruit of love, was so predominant in these believers that it caused them to forget about their own needs and look only at the needs of others.

And of the rest durst no man join himself to them: but the people magnified them. And believers were the more added to the Lord, multitudes both of men and women. Insomuch that they brought forth the sick into the streets, and laid them on beds and couches, that at the least the shadow of Peter passing by might overshadow some of them. There came also a multitude out of the cities round about unto Jerusalem, bringing sick folks, and them which were vexed with unclean spirits: and they were healed every one (vv. 13-16).

Multitudes of people were getting saved and healed! When there are multitudes from areas north, south, east, and west of Jerusalem, plus those in the city being healed—it is a work of great grace. This only happened a few times in the ministry of Jesus. The grace of giving moved upon the hearts of the people. People were being healed, delivered, and set free from demon spirits. In the midst of that, however, was the sudden death of Ananias and Sapphira, as a consequence of lying to the Holy Spirit. ***There was a flow of grace and judgment at the same time.***

---

[1]Brethren, Acts 4:33, Power Bible CD 5.6

Grace vs. Judgment

Chapter Three

The Spiritual Law of Judgment

We've looked at the word "grace" and its definitions, the flow of great grace, and the operation of judgment in the Book of Acts. In this chapter, let's take a closer look at the word "judgment".

Be not deceived; God is not mocked: for whatsoever a man soweth, that shall he also reap. For he that soweth to his flesh shall of the flesh reap corruption; but he that soweth to the Spirit shall of the Spirit reap life everlasting. And let us not be weary in well doing: for in due season we shall reap, if we faint not (Galatians 6:7-9).

Galatians was written to the church of Galatia—to believers, not sinners. Notice the phrase: "*whatsoever a man soweth.*" We can sow something that brings a good harvest, or we can sow something that brings a bad harvest. This same principle has been in place from the very beginning of time. Genesis 8:22 says, "*While the earth remaineth, seedtime and harvest, and cold and heat, and summer and winter, and day and night shall not cease.*"

Our harvest is determined by what we plant with our actions, our words, our money, and our lives. In other words, judgment is neutral. Judgment is only the fulfillment of the Scripture. If we sow to life, we will receive life. If we sow to death, we will receive death. That's the law of judgment (Galatians 6:8).

As I said earlier, the word "judge" means to conclude or decree, to try or determine. In a trial, the verdict is either innocent or guilty. A judgment in a trial doesn't necessarily mean that the defendant is going to jail. That person could be innocent and have all the charges against him dropped. A judgment is simply a determination that can go either way. A judgment is the final result of the cycle of seedtime and harvest.

If a nation plants seeds to the flesh and sin, God's Word would be void if there wasn't a harvest of negative judgment. If a nation, or a person, plants seeds in line with the Word of God, the Word would be void if it did not produce the blessing.

Therefore, it's not a matter of all grace or all judgment; they're both operating in the same place. If you hear a minister or a church taking an extreme position one way or the other, that in itself should tell you that it's not a Biblical position. It's not taking the totality of the Word into account.

The Law of Seedtime and Harvest

Hebrews 4:16 begins with the word "therefore," which means that we need to go back and see what it is "there for." In other words, we need to determine the context that allows for the truth in this verse. We could go back to verse one, which also begins with the words, "Let us therefore" taking us back to the previous chapter. I would encourage you to study this on your own, but for our purposes here, let's begin reading at verse 10: *"For he that is entered into his rest, he also hath ceased from his own works, as God did from his."*

Hebrews 4:2 says that the children of Israel didn't enter into that rest because of fear; they didn't mix any faith with the Word so they didn't cross over into the Promised Land, God's rest or place of provision for them. The men who went into the Promised Land came back and said, "That land is like God said it was! It's a land of milk and honey! It is laden with grapes!" The only negative thing was that they had walled cities and there were giants in the land.

God has a Promised Land, a place of milk and honey, set aside and anointed for us! But we must remember that anytime we obey God and go where He sends us, there will be giants. Stop crying about the giants! They come with the territory. The Word says that if we get a hundredfold return, we will also get persecution with it (Mark 10:30). Satan is not going to lie down; he's not going to let everybody see us blessed so they will come running to our Jesus! He's going to try to make us back down. That's why he uses affliction, persecution, cares of this world, deceitfulness of riches, and lusts of other things to try and choke the Word out of our lives (see Mark 4). He wants to make the Word unfruitful so we won't be an example of God's blessing to everybody else.

If we fly on an airplane, there's a law of lift in place that keeps the plane in the air. If we delete any of that law, we will find that another law goes into effect—the law of gravity. The reason it's called a law is because it works every time! So don't say, "Why did God allow this to happen?" There's a spiritual law of judgment in place. God's not sitting on His throne saying, "I think I'm going to torment so-and-so today." No, there are laws that are in play—the law of seedtime and harvest.

God has given us His Word and His Spirit. God warns us when we are about to run into a wall. He'll send prophets; He'll send other men and women of God to tell us what the consequences of our actions will be. God always warns His people so we won't get into the negative judgment.

Judgment from Actions

Let's look at one more thing:

Wherefore whosoever shall eat this bread, and drink this cup of the Lord, unworthily, shall be guilty of the body and blood of the Lord. But let a man examine himself, and so let him eat of that bread, and drink of that cup (1 Corinthians 11:27-28).

This is written to the church at Corinth. This is the church that is filled with the Holy Ghost, full of the gifts of the Spirit (see 1 Corinthians 1:5).

For he that eateth and drinketh unworthily, eateth and drinketh damnation [judgment] to himself, not discerning the

Lord's body. For this cause many are weak and sickly among
you, and many sleep (vv. 29-31).

In these verses, Paul answers the question: **"Why does God**
allows certain things to happen?" God did not cause these things
to happen. Notice the verse says, *"For this cause many are weak and*
sickly among you, and many sleep." It's not God's fault, and it's not the
local church's fault. People determine what judgment they receive
by their own actions—by eating and drinking unworthily.

Many in this tongue-talking, Spirit-filled church—founded,
taught, and raised by the Apostle Paul—were sick. Why? Because
they didn't rightly discern the body. *"For if we would judge ourselves,*
we should not be judged. But when we are judged, we are chastened of
the Lord, that we should not be condemned with the world" (v. 32). The
word "chastened" means instructed of the Lord.

Right Standing

Thank God that His power is available to us. Grace is unmerited
favor, but if you want to use one term for the grace of God, it would
be "the power of God." The Holy Ghost is power Himself.

Let us labour therefore to enter into that rest, lest any man fall
after the same example of unbelief. For the word of God is quick
[alive], and powerful, and sharper than any twoedged sword,
piercing even to the dividing asunder of soul and spirit, and of
the joints and marrow, and is a discerner of the thoughts and
intents of the heart. Neither is there any creature that is not

*manifest in his sight: but all things are naked and opened unto
the eyes of him with whom we have to do (Hebrews 4:11-13).*

The Word of God is a living thing. The Word of God is active.
The Word of God is powerful. The Word of God is sharper than
any double-edged sword. It's a discerner of the thoughts and intents
of the heart. Jesus is the Word; there is nothing that is not manifest
in His sight.

*Seeing then [since that's true] that we have a great high
priest, that is passed into the heavens, Jesus the Son of God,
let us hold fast our profession. For we have not an high priest
which cannot be touched with the feeling of our infirmities; but
was in all points tempted like as we are, yet without sin. Let
us therefore come boldly unto the throne of grace, that we may
obtain mercy, and find grace to help in time of need (Hebrews
4:14-16).*

The High Priest's job was to take a sacrifice into the Holy of
Holies once a year and offer up the blood of that sacrifice to cover
the peoples' sins for a year. But Jesus isn't just the Chief Priest of
the law; He is the One and only One, who offered Himself once
and for all—for all sins, for all time. He is the Great Priest who
offered His blood before the Father.

New Creation

The blood washed away our sins and we became children of
God. Our status was changed once we became born again: *"For he*

hath made him to be sin for us, who knew no sin; that we might be made the righteousness of God in him" (*2 Corinthians 5:21*). We became in right standing with God. God said we **were** a sinner, and now we **are** a saint. We were lost, but now we are found. We were going to Hell, and now we are going to Heaven.

In John 3, Jesus said that we must be born again. Nicodemus said, "How can I be born again? Can I go back into my mother's womb and be born?"

Jesus responded by saying, "You're a teacher, and you don't know this?" "*For God so loved the world, that he gave his only begotten Son, that whosoever believeth in him should not perish, but have everlasting life*" (*John 3:16*). Yes, you received eternal life. But that wasn't all that happened, just because you believed.

Therefore if any man be in Christ, he is a new creature: old things are passed away; behold, all things are become new (2 Corinthians 5:17).

The word "new" means something that never existed before, is now here. Not only did God change your status, but He also made you an entirely new creation. The most important miracle, and the greatest operation of power that ever happened, took place on that day. We were born in this world with the nature of sin, but when we acknowledged Jesus as our Lord and Savior, the Holy Ghost came. He didn't renovate us; He didn't take something old and fix it up a little bit. The man or woman who was in our body died, and the Holy Ghost created a whole new person with the power of God. We are a new creation; the old is passed away, and everything is new. That is the work of grace!

> *Seeing then that we have a great high priest, that is passed into the heavens, Jesus the Son of God, let us hold fast our profession. For we have not an high priest which cannot be touched with the feeling of our infirmities; but was in all points tempted like as we are, yet without sin. Let us therefore come boldly unto the throne of grace, that we may obtain mercy, and find grace to help in time of need (Hebrews 4:14-16).*

If we have sin, we can come to the High Priest. Grace will help us!

> *If we confess* [acknowledge] *our sins, he is faithful and just to forgive us our sins, and to cleanse us from all unrighteousness (1 John 1:9, emphasis mine).*

John is writing to the church because in the next chapter he says, "*My little children, these things write I unto you, that ye sin not. And if any man sin, we have an advocate with the Father, Jesus Christ the righteous: and he is the propitiation for our sins: and not for ours only, but also for the sins of the whole world*" *(1 John 2:1-2).* The only thing we have to do is confess, or acknowledge, our sin.

You can come boldly before God! Yes, you have a problem—and yes, you messed up. But at the throne of grace, God will see you and have compassion on you. He will provide you with the power to overcome any sin in your life. The power of God will help you overcome the sin which does so easily beset you (see Hebrews 12:1).

The grace, the power, of God will help you overcome that problem, malady, or issue—whatever it is—so that it will no longer have a hold on you. You can be free because of the power of the grace of Almighty God!

Grace vs. Judgment

Chapter Four

God's Graciousness for Grace

We have defined the terms "grace" and "judgment". We have also seen the importance of this information in determining how these words are used in context, and how to correctly apply them to our lives. We have taken a tour of Scripture to look at many of the uses of the word "grace," and we have identified which definition is applicable. We have also looked at Acts Chapter 4, a situation where not only did great grace abound, but also judgment was meted out, proving that both grace and judgment can be operating in the same place.

In this chapter, let's look more specifically at the first definition of the word "grace" [*charis*] in Strong's Exhaustive Concordance—graciousness. Then we will explore some more definitions. The word "graciousness" means kind, condescension, voluntary descent from rank or dignity or a just claim.

And the Word was made flesh, and dwelt among us, (and we beheld his glory, the glory as of the only begotten of the Father,) full of grace and truth. John bare witness of him, and cried, saying, This was he of whom I spake, He that cometh after me is preferred before me: for he was before me. (John 1:14-15).

The Holy Spirit is the Spirit of grace. The anointing on Jesus was the Spirit, full of grace. John goes on to say, *"And of his fulness have all we received, and grace for grace" (v. 16).*

Graciousness as Fullness

Let's look at this fullness from the perspective of Ephesians Chapter 1. In this chapter, notice that God has blessed us with all spiritual blessings in Christ Jesus (v. 3). He has chosen us from the foundation of the world (v. 4). We have redemption and forgiveness of sins *"according to the riches of his grace" (v. 7)*. The word "riches" in the Greek is *ploutos*, which means wealth as fullness, a valuable bestowment. The word "grace" means graciousness.

"Wherein he hath abounded toward us in all wisdom and prudence" (v. 8). In other words, God has poured out all His fullness—all His graciousness—on us. The riches of His grace have been poured out in wisdom. We are sealed with the Holy Spirit of promise (v. 13), the down payment of our inheritance (v. 14).

Paul continues:

Wherefore I also, after I heard of your faith in the Lord Jesus, and love unto all the saints, cease not to give thanks for you, making mention of you in my prayers (vv. 15-16).

What was his prayer?

That the God of our Lord Jesus Christ, the Father of glory, may give unto you the spirit of wisdom and revelation in the knowledge of him: The eyes of your understanding being enlightened; that ye may know what is the hope of his calling, and what the riches of the glory of his inheritance in the saints, and what is the exceeding greatness of his power to us-ward who believe, according to the working of his mighty power, which he wrought in Christ, when he raised him from the dead (vv. 17-20).

In other words, Paul says, "I don't want you to be ignorant. I want you to have knowledge and information, so I'm praying the Father will give you the Spirit of wisdom and revelation in the knowledge of Him. I'm praying that the eyes of your understanding will be enlightened so that you will come to know the riches [*ploutos*] of the glory. I am praying that you will know wealth as fullness, that the Spirit will bestow what is valuable on you." Therefore, the *riches of the glory* is something that is given to us, something that is bestowed, poured out, or placed on us. The riches of the glory of His inheritance belong to the saints.

God's power is exceedingly great. The word "exceeding" in the Greek is *huperballo*, which means to far surpass the usual mark. Paul wants us to know the magnitude of His power to us who believe, a power that is according to the working [*energeia*] of His mighty force and strength. The Greek word for power is *kratos*—the same power that God used when He raised Jesus from the dead.

...and set him at his own right hand in the heavenly places, far above all principality, and power, and might, and dominion, and every name that is named, not only in this world, but also in that which is to come: And hath put all things under his feet, and gave him to be the head over all things to the church, which is his body, the fulness of him that filleth all in all (vv. 20-23).

The Greek word for "fulness" is pleroma, which means completion, content, supplement, performance, or fulfilling. The church is the completion of Jesus. He's the head; we're the body. In a physical sense, the rest of the body—the torso, arms, legs, feet—all of it—completes the head, so there will be an entire body. Likewise, the church is the body—the completion, the supplement, the performance, the fulfilling *"of him that filleth all in all."*

The word "filleth" means to cram a net full until you can't get any more in it. In other words, Jesus is everywhere; He's in all, and the fullness of Him, the Church, is supposed to be everywhere, filling every place where there is not complete knowledge of the Lord Jesus Christ.

Believer, you are a filler! You are a completer! *"And of his fulness have all we received, and grace for grace" (John 1:16).* If you are a member of the body of Christ, you have received His content; you complete Him. You have received His *graciousness for grace*: you have received His power!

Graciousness as Inheritance

Now, let's take this a little further.

And now, brethren, I commend you to God, and to the word of his grace, which is able to build you up, and to give you an inheritance among all them which are sanctified (Acts 20:32).

The *word of his graciousness* is able to build us up and give us an inheritance among all those who are sanctified. We can read about this inheritance in Ephesians 1. The inheritance is the Holy Spirit. He is the grace. He is the riches in glory.

Romans 1:16-17 tells us more about what the Word is: "*For I am not ashamed of the gospel of Christ: for it is the power of God unto salvation to every one that believeth; to the Jew first, and also to the Greek. For therein is the righteousness of God revealed from faith to faith: as it is written, The just shall live by faith.*"

The Gospel of Christ is the Word of God, the power of God unto salvation [deliverance], to everyone that believeth, to the Jew first and also to the Greek. The righteousness of God is revealed, the cover is taken off—from faith to faith. The Word is the power of God, and the power of God is the Holy Spirit. The Holy Spirit is the grace of God. He is not a statistic; He is not a place—He is a person.

Graciousness as Action

Where do you find the graciousness of God? Who kindly condescended to humankind? Who bowed down? Who voluntarily gave up His rank? Who voluntarily gave up His dignity? Who gave up His just claim?

Philippians 2 says: *"Let this mind be in you, which was also in Christ Jesus: Who, being in the form of God, thought it not robbery to be equal with God" (v. 5-6)*. This is how Jesus thought, which means that He was not ashamed to say, "I am the Son of God." Believer, you should not be ashamed to say, "I am the son or daughter of God." As believers, we should think the same way He does. In other words, we should have the same attitude as Jesus.

John 1:12 says, *"But as many as received him, to them gave he power [authority, right, and privilege] to become the sons of God, even to them that believe on his name" (emphasis mine)*.

Jesus didn't shrink from anything, because He was the Son of God. He certainly didn't shrink from the devil. And because we are sons and daughters of God, we should not shrink from anything. We certainly should not shrink from the devil!

But made himself of no reputation, and took upon him the form of a servant, and was made in the likeness of men: And being found in fashion as a man, he humbled himself, and became obedient unto death, even the death of the cross (Philippians 2:7-8).

Jesus took upon Himself the form of a servant. The word "servant" comes from the Greek word *doulos*, which means slave—a person who has no rights. This was God's graciousness in action.

Graciousness as Gift

What shall we say then that Abraham our father, as pertaining to the flesh, hath found? For if Abraham were justified by works, he hath whereof to glory; but not before God. For what saith the scripture? Abraham believed God, and it was counted unto him for righteousness. Now to him that worketh is the reward not reckoned of grace, but of debt (Romans 4:1-4).

Paul is explaining righteousness to these people. The word "debt" here means gift. If I offer you my money clip and you reach out and take it, that's a gift. You didn't do anything to earn it. You didn't fast, pray, shout, or offer sacrifices. You just received it. So now, all you need to do is give thanks and this will open the door for you to receive more.

Remember, one of the definitions of "grace" is gift. Before Jesus took our place on the cross and died for our sins, a priest had to offer sacrifices for the sins of the people. If people were able to get into heaven because of works, then they would do so because God owed them. Yet Paul says, "No, God's never going to be in your debt. He's going to give you grace, a gift."

Therefore it is of faith, that it might be by grace [or the gifting to you]; to the end the promise might be sure to all the seed (v. 16a, emphasis mine).

You must believe for it rather than work for it.

Therefore [as a result of believing rather than working for it] being justified by faith, we have peace with God through our Lord Jesus Christ: By whom also we have access by faith into this grace wherein we stand, and rejoice in hope of the glory of God (Romans 5:1-2, emphasis mine).

Therefore being declared righteous, made innocent or justified by faith [*pistis*], by trust, you have prosperity, quietness and rest or peace with God through our Lord Jesus Christ. The word "Lord", *kyriou*, means master or controller. With many Christians, Jesus is only their Savior, not their Lord. But when He is Lord of your life, He controls you. If He says, "Go to Denmark," you go. You don't say, "What about this," because that would put you in control. But He is the Lord Jesus Christ — your Supreme Authority, Controller, Master, and Savior. He is anointed to give you access by your trust, confidence, and belief into this grace, this gift, wherein you abide and rejoice in confident expectation of the glory to God. Why? Because you received the gift! Look at verse 8 (this is one of my favorite verses):

But God commendeth [introduced] his love toward us, in that, while we were yet sinners, Christ died for us. Much more then, being now justified by his blood, we shall be saved from wrath through him (vv. 8-9, emphasis mine).

Jesus is the door to life!

Nevertheless death reigned from Adam to Moses, even over them that had not sinned after the similitude of Adam's transgression, who is the figure [model] *of him that was to come* (v. 14, emphasis mine).

Adam, the first man, was the model of the one coming—the second Adam. First Corinthians 15 says that Jesus is the second Adam. *"But not as the offence, so also is the free gift. For if through the offence of one many be dead, much more the grace of God, and the gift of grace, which is by one man, Jesus Christ, hath abounded unto many"* *(Romans 5:15).* Jesus became obedient unto death. When He died, His blood was shed—and we were justified by His blood (Romans 5: 9). He lowered Himself, took upon humankind's flesh, and obeyed the Father by shedding His blood on the cross for us. If we believe in the blood and receive the graciousness, we can stand against everything that hell has to offer.

Notice Paul's emphasis on the gift of God: *"so is the gift!"* The free gift!

... much more the grace [graciousness] *of God, and the gift by grace, which is by one man, Jesus Christ, hath abounded unto many. And not as it was by one that sinned, so is the gift: for the judgment was by one to condemnation, but the free gift* [grace] *is of many offences unto justification. For if by one man's offence death reigned by one; much more they which*

receive abundance of grace and of the gift of righteousness shall reign in life by one, Jesus Christ [the anointed One]) (vv. 15b-17, emphasis mine)

Death ruled because of Adam's disobedience. But this wasn't the final word. Notice Paul's comparison—much more! The force of God's gift is much greater than the force that enslaved man and put him in the slave market of sin. That force of sin doomed man, but God Almighty in the person of the Holy Ghost—the very grace of God—was greater!

"Much more they which receive abundance of grace." The Greek word for abundance means super abundance. We don't just receive some of the gift. We accept all of the gifts and power. We receive abundance of grace and the gift of righteousness. Notice that the grace is not righteousness. Again, we can't use these words interchangeably.

Therefore as by the offence of one judgment came upon all men to condemnation; even so by the righteousness of one [Jesus] the free gift came upon all men unto justification of life. For as by one man's disobedience many were made sinners, so by the obedience of one shall many be made righteous. Moreover the law entered, that the offence might abound. But where sin abounded, grace did much more abound (Romans 5:18-20, emphasis mine).

God saw the condition of man. What He told Adam had come to pass: *"for in the day that thou eatest thereof thou shalt surely die" (Genesis 2:17)*. Although Adam didn't lose his natural life for 930 more years, he entered a state of spiritual death, having Satan's nature and experiencing separation from God. God saw that sin was growing, so His graciousness to us grew. The worse things became, the greater His graciousness became!

That as sin hath reigned unto death, even so might grace reign through righteousness unto eternal life by Jesus Christ our Lord (Romans 5:21).

Look at this again: Grace reigned through the door of right standing unto eternal life by Jesus Christ.

What shall we say then? Shall we continue in sin, that grace may abound? God forbid. How shall we, that are dead to sin, live any longer therein? (Romans 6:1-2).

Shall you stay in sin simply because God is gracious? No. Just because God is kind, doesn't mean you should stay in sin.

For sin shall not have dominion over you: for ye are not under the law, but under grace (v. 14).

You're under that free gift!

What then? shall we sin, because we are not under the law, but under grace? God forbid. Know ye not, that to whom ye yield yourselves servants to obey, his servants ye are to whom ye obey; whether of sin unto death, or of obedience unto righteousness? (vv. 15-16).

Paul is talking about judgment. The word "yield" means to stand beside. In other words, he's saying that the one we stand next to is the one we will receive. The one we yield to is the one we will be hooked up to. If we yield to obedience, we will receive righteousness. If we yield to sin, we will receive death. In other words, we can receive the gift offered to us, or we can decide to go with the devil. Our judgment can be negative or positive. The determinate is us. We make the choice!

Chapter Five

Grace in Specific Contexts

W e have looked at the word "grace" in several verses to identify many definitions, and in this chapter, we will explore in greater detail, God's grace in specific contexts such as giving, liberty, and salvation. In addition, we will see that grace is God's pleasure.

In 2 Peter 1, Peter says, "*Grace and peace be multiplied unto you through the knowledge of God, and of Jesus our Lord. According as his divine power hath given unto us all things that pertain unto life and godliness, through the knowledge of him that hath called us to glory and virtue*" *(vv. 2-3)*.

The word "knowledge" in the Greek is *epignosis*, which means full, complete, and exact knowledge. In other words, the more we know about the Father and the more we know about the Son, the more we will understand the benefits that have been ascribed to us. Those benefits are the promises of God!

Grace as Giving

We have already seen how Paul persuaded the church of Corinth to join in the grace of giving like the church in Macedonia, a church that gave out of their deep poverty, but let's take a look again:

Moreover, brethren, we do you to wit of the grace of God bestowed on the churches of Macedonia; how that in a great trial of affliction the abundance of their joy and their deep poverty abounded unto the riches of their liberality (2 Corinthians 8:1-2).

Notice that grace is something that God bestows—something that is put on us. These people were not only in poverty, they were in deep poverty. In times of deep poverty, the tendency is to stop giving. Yet, the church in Macedonia's response to severe financial problems was to give more. It didn't make sense in the natural, but it made spiritual sense. At one of the churches I pastor, we have increased our giving to those outside our walls. Whenever the devil messes with our finances, we just increase our giving even more!

For to their power, I bear record, yea, and beyond their power they were willing of themselves; praying us with much intreaty that we would receive the gift, and take upon us the fellowship of the ministering to the saints (vv. 3-4).

Paul is telling the church at Corinth, "You all need to be like these people in Macedonia!"

For as touching the ministering to the saints, it is superfluous for me to write to you: For I know the forwardness of your mind, for which I boast of you to them of Macedonia, that Achaia was ready a year ago; and your zeal hath provoked very many. Yet have I sent the brethren, lest our boasting of you should be in vain in this behalf; that, as I said, ye may be ready (2 Corinthians 9:1-3).

They haven't done anything yet, but Paul is bragging about them.

Lest haply if they of Macedonia come with me, and find you unprepared, we (that we say not, ye) should be ashamed in this same confident boasting. Therefore I thought it necessary to exhort the brethren, that they would go before unto you, and make up beforehand your bounty, whereof ye had notice before, that the same might be ready, as a matter of bounty, and not as of covetousness (vv. 4-5).

The word "bounty" here is largesse, and is defined as something that is given generously; liberality in giving: generosity. Paul is referring to their offering. All of these Scriptures from Second Corinthians 8 and 9, form the context for what follows:

But this I say, He which soweth sparingly shall reap also sparingly; and he which soweth bountifully shall reap also bountifully. Every man according as he purposeth in his heart, so let him give; not grudgingly, or of necessity: for God loveth a cheerful giver. And God is able to make all grace abound toward you; that ye, always having all sufficiency in all things, may abound to every good work (vv. 6-8).

The word "grace" here means benefit. God is able to make all benefits abound to us when we give much, instead of little. Paul is telling the church of Corinth what is going to happen to the church at Macedonia. He says, "I've been bragging about you, so don't embarrass me when I come with the brothers of the church of Macedonia who gave out of their deep poverty, only to find that you're unprepared to give." Remember, they didn't have cars or the Internet; they only had donkeys. So Paul wasn't going to see them for a while. He was just giving them an advance order. Always—always—read Scripture in context!

If we receive all of God's benefits, we're going to have all sufficiency and all satisfaction in everything—so we may abound, or excel, to every good deed. God's benefits aren't only for us. He gives to us out of His bounty, so we can do something with it.

As it is written, He hath dispersed abroad; he hath given to the poor: his righteousness remaineth for ever. Now he that ministereth seed to the sower both minister bread for your food, and multiply your seed sown, and increase the fruits of your righteousness (vv. 9-10).

God's the one who gave us what we have. He's the sower. He gave us the seed, and He will multiply the seed that **is** sown—not the seed that is **not** sown. The Greek word for "seed" is *sperma*. When a man plants sperm into a woman and that sperm fertilizes her egg, after a certain amount of time, there will be a harvest of a baby!

Being enriched in every thing to all bountifulness, which causeth through us thanksgiving to God (v. 11).

Paul is saying that when we plant seed into the ground, a judgment will happen. When we plant seed from a right spirit and a right heart for the right purpose, the benefits of God will go to work for us. The judgment will be a harvest of blessing that will increase the results of our righteousness, and we will be made rich in everything.

Scripture records many places where it says we reap all the benefits of God from a single action. That's how powerful giving is! No wonder the devil fights us so hard on the issue of giving.

And by their prayer for you, which long after you for the exceeding grace of God in you. Thanks be unto God for his unspeakable gift (vv. 14-15).

The exceeding grace of God in them was their giving, their liberality [one of the definitions for grace]. We need to see the word "grace" from the vantage point of the totality of Scripture. We can pick a verse here and there, but we need to see Scripture in a large context.

Grace as Liberty

Let's look at another use of the word "grace".

Stand fast therefore in the liberty wherewith Christ hath made us free, and be not entangled again with the yoke of bondage (Galatians 5:1).

Paul was talking to Jewish Christians who still wanted to bind up everyone. This desire to entangle people—this position of bondage—has continued throughout the centuries. Pastor Deborah and I grew up in a church where the men could dress sharp, wearing whatever they wanted, but the women had to wear black dresses that reached the floor. Furthermore, the women couldn't do anything to make themselves look good—no makeup, no hair coloring—nothing.

God isn't against makeup! Enjoy yourself. Just don't become so full of yourself that you spend all of your time and money on your looks. Don't dress like Jezebel either. Pay attention to the way you look, but don't spend more time on your appearance than you do with God and His Word.

Behold, I Paul say unto you, that if ye be circumcised, Christ shall profit you nothing. For I testify again to every man that is circumcised, that he is a debtor to do the whole law (Galatians 5:2-3).

The Jewish Christians were trying to make Gentile believers get circumcised, but Paul told them that if they followed this part of the law, they needed to follow all of the law. James 2:10 says that if we violate one article of the law, then we are guilty of breaking it all.

Christ is become of no effect unto you, whosoever of you are justified by the law; ye are fallen from grace (v. 4).

In other words, we are fallen from the gift. Paul is talking about works and gifts, not about status. We don't have to work for grace.

Grace as Salvation

Titus 2:11 says, *"For the grace of God that bringeth salvation hath appeared to all men."* The word salvation is *soteria*, which means deliverance. The grace of God is the gift that brings our salvation and deliverance.

Ephesians 1 talks about the Holy Spirit who is in us and on us; He's the down payment, the riches of glory. We are the fullness. Then, Paul says, *"And you hath he quickened, who were dead in trespasses and sins" (Ephesians 2:1).* We were once dead in trespasses and sins, but God has made us alive!

Wherein in time past ye walked according to the course of this world, according to the prince of the power of the air, the spirit that now worketh in the children of disobedience: Among whom also we all had our conversation [lifestyle] in times past in the lusts of our flesh, fulfilling the desires of the flesh and of the mind; and were by nature the children of wrath, even as others. But God, who is rich in mercy, for his great love wherewith he loved us, Even when we were dead in sins, hath quickened us together with Christ, (by grace ye are saved;) (vv. 2-5, emphasis mine).

In other words, Paul is saying, "Church at Galatia, God has made you alive with the anointing and with the Anointed One. You are saved by grace!"

This word "grace" means the work of God. When we were born again, we didn't just experience a change in status from sinner to saint. A work of God, a work of the Holy Spirit, took place in our lives. What was the status of righteous men and women in the Old Testament who weren't yet able to benefit from the death and resurrection of Jesus? Saints in the Old Testament didn't go to heaven when they died. Let's take a look at the story of a rich man and Lazarus to see where these saints went:

> *There was a certain rich man, which was clothed in purple and fine linen, and fared sumptuously every day: And there was a certain beggar named Lazarus, which was laid at his gate, full of sores, and desiring to be fed with the crumbs which fell from the rich man's table: moreover the dogs came and licked his sores. And it came to pass, that the beggar died, and was carried by the angels into Abraham's bosom: the rich man also died, and was buried; and in hell he lift up his eyes, being in torments, and seeth Abraham afar off, and Lazarus in his bosom. And he cried and said, Father Abraham, have mercy on me, and send Lazarus, that he may dip the tip of his finger in water, and cool my tongue; for I am tormented in this flame (Luke 16:19-24).*

The Word says, "a certain rich man." Every time we see the word "certain," that means the particular story is not a parable. So in this instance, this man actually lived. Notice that he still had a bad attitude after his death and was asking for someone to serve him.

> *But Abraham said, Son, remember that thou in thy lifetime received thy good things, and likewise Lazarus evil things: but now he is comforted, and thou art tormented. And beside all this, between us and you there is a great gulf fixed: so that they which would pass from hence to you cannot; neither can they pass to us, that would come from thence (vv. 25-26).*

Then the rich man said, "Send somebody to my five brothers so they don't end up here as well." Abraham said, "They have Moses and the prophets. They won't hear them, and they won't hear anyone else as well, even though that person was raised from the dead."

Here's the point. The place called Abraham's bosom was where all the Old Testament saints went after they died. Abraham, Isaac, Jacob, Moses, David, and all the prophets didn't initially go to heaven; they went to a place called "Abraham's bosom," in the center of the earth.

Ephesians 4:7 says, "*But unto every one of us is given grace according to the measure of the gift of Christ [according to the measure of the anointing].*" The word "grace" means the manifested measure of the Holy Spirit that every one of us has.

> *Wherefore he saith, When he ascended up on high, he led captivity captive, and gave gifts unto men (v. 8).*

When Jesus ascended, He "led captivity captive." This means

that a great multitude of the captives were with Him. These were the Old Testament saints who were in faith, believing for a promise that had not yet come to pass. In fact, it was a mystery to them how God was going to do it, yet, they believed anyway.

> *(Now that he ascended, what is it but that he also descended first into the lower parts of the earth? He that descended is the same also that ascended up far above all heavens, that he might fill all things.) And he gave some, apostles; and some, prophets; and some, evangelists; and some, pastors and teachers (vv. 9-11).*

Those Old Testament saints didn't go to heaven until the completion of God's plan, when Jesus rose from the grave on the third day. In the story of the rich man and Lazarus, notice they could see one another across the great gulf. This is why in Acts 2:31, Peter talked about David seeing Jesus in the pit of hell. David saw Him there. But on the third day, grace Himself—the Holy Ghost—energized Jesus and raised Him from the dead. Jesus threw off principalities and powers, and He beat Satan, making an open display of him—dragging him down and triumphing over him in that defeat. I wish I could have been there to see that beat-down! I bet David was dancing out of his clothes again!

Only when Jesus was raised from the dead, could people be born again. Jesus said that unless a man be born again, he cannot enter the kingdom of heaven (see John 3:3). Jesus completed the Gospel—and the saints believed and were saved.

As we've seen, two things happen when we get saved. First, we receive our status change from unrighteous to righteous. Second Corinthians 5:21 says, "For he hath made him to be sin for us, who knew no sin; that we might be made the righteousness of God in him." If that was all that happened, however, we would be no different than the Old Testament saints. Look at what else happened: "Therefore if any man be in Christ, he is a new creature: old things are passed away; behold, all things are become new" (2 Corinthians 5:17).

We become a new creation. We become a being that didn't exist before. We are saved by grace. The power that raised Jesus from the dead also raised us from the dead. The power that defeated the devil, defeated him again, to save us.

> *Even when we were dead in sins, hath quickened us together with Christ, (by grace ye are saved;) and hath raised us up together, and made us sit together in heavenly places in Christ Jesus: That in the ages to come he might shew the exceeding riches of his grace* [ploutos: his wealth as fullness, his valuable bestowment] *in his kindness toward us through Christ Jesus. For by grace are ye saved through faith; and that not of yourselves: it is the gift of God: Not of works, lest any man should boast. For we are his workmanship, created in Christ Jesus unto good works, which God hath before ordained that we should walk in them (Ephesians 2:5-10, emphasis mine).*

Paul says it again: "*for by grace are ye saved.*" Paul has been talking about that grace from the beginning of Ephesians.

Grace as Pleasure

In 2 Timothy 1:8-9, Paul says, "*Be not thou therefore ashamed of the testimony of our Lord, nor of me his prisoner: but be thou partaker of the afflictions of the gospel according to the power of God; Who hath saved us, and called us with an holy calling, not according to our works, but according to his own purpose and grace, which was given us in Christ Jesus before the world began.*"

This word grace means pleasure. Remember Isaiah 53:10 says, "*Yet it pleased the LORD to bruise him; he hath put him to grief:* when thou shalt make his soul an offering for sin, he shall see his seed, he shall prolong his days, and the pleasure of the LORD shall prosper in his hand.*" God prospered, and the fulfilling of His plan gave Him pleasure.

First Timothy 2:4 says the same thing: "*Who will have all men to be saved, and to come unto the knowledge of the truth.*" God wills that all men be saved. That's what gives God pleasure. When we have the right Word for the right situation, the Word makes perfect sense. It isn't confusing.

Believers, you must hear the whole message. Place yourself under the care of a father in the faith who rightly divides the Word. Once again, when you know the definition, when you take time to determine the context, and when you know the audience that the writer is talking to, you'll see that the meaning absolutely fits!

Chapter Six

A Tour of God's Covenant of Grace

God doesn't sit on the throne and say, "I don't like you anymore so I'm taking you out." Rather, as we've seen, judgment is a fulfilling of a spiritual law of harvest that says that we reap what we sow—an agricultural analogy. To sow means to plant seed in the ground, and to reap means to get a return of the same thing that we planted. If we plant apple seeds, we will not get a harvest of oranges or watermelons. I don't care how much we fast, pray, shout, or scream about it—the law of reaping says that what we sow will come to pass.

> *Be not deceived; God is not mocked: for whatsoever a man soweth, that shall he also reap. For he that soweth to his flesh shall of the flesh reap corruption; but he that soweth to the Spirit shall of the Spirit reap life everlasting (Galatians 6:7-8).*

The Greek word for life is *zoe*, which means eternal life, or life as God has it. The determinate of judgment is what we sow. Judgment is not all negative—we only reap corruption if we sow to the flesh. If we sow to the Spirit, we reap something positive—life everlasting.

God's instructions to the children of Israel illustrate how judgment is determined by our actions.

> *And it shall come to pass, if thou shalt hearken diligently unto the voice of the LORD thy God, to observe and to do all his commandments which I command thee this day, that the LORD thy God will set thee on high above all nations of the earth: And all these blessings shall come on thee, and overtake thee, if thou shalt hearken unto the voice of the LORD thy God (Deuteronomy 28:1-2).*

This is followed by a list of blessings for keeping His commandments: blessed in the city, blessed in the field, blessed in the basket, blessed in the store, blessed coming in, and blessed going out.

> *But it shall come to pass, if thou wilt not hearken unto the voice of the LORD thy God, to observe to do all his commandments and his statutes which I command thee this day; that all these curses shall come upon thee, and overtake thee (Deuteronomy 28:15).*

This is followed by a list of curses that the Israelites will reap if they fail to keep God's commandments: cursed in the city, cursed in the field, cursed in the basket, and cursed in the store.

In Matthew 5:18, Jesus says that every letter of the Word of God will come to pass because it has integrity and is spiritual law:

"For verily I say unto you, Till heaven and earth pass, one jot or one tittle shall in no wise pass from the law, till all be fulfilled."

The word "jot" in the Greek is *iota*, the smallest letter of the Greek alphabet. The word "tittle," *keraia*, means a little horn—possibly a distinguishing apostrophe on letters—the least particle. The word "law" is *nomos*, referring to the Mosaic Law. In other words, Jesus said that every single letter, every single particle of the Word of God, will come to pass. That's why the Book of Revelation says that we better not add to the Scripture or take away from it (Revelation 22:18-19). There's judgment if we do this, because every single part of the Word will come to pass!

Of course, the consequences of the laws of God can be mitigated some and the time from sowing to reaping can be expanded some, but the bottom line is that if we plant a certain seed, we will eventually reap the harvest. Once again, judgment can go both ways—good or bad.

Scripture doesn't teach us that we are living in an era of all grace that overturns the laws of judgment. God has spoken in a number of ways, including through His prophets and books, to tell the church and the nation what is happening. He always warns us about what is ahead. He will tell us what road we're on and what seed we've planted. And if we keep planting this kind of seed, we will have this kind of harvest.

Victory over Death and Manifested Love

God gave me a special message to deliver for New Year's 2014. He wanted me to tell His people about what was coming. He wanted believers to know that when the negative side of judgment starts manifesting, when the full fruit of harvest comes, the body of Christ can have victory over death and experience manifested love from God. Notice what produces the manifested love of God.

He that hath my commandments, and keepeth them, he it is that loveth me: and he that loveth me shall be loved of my Father, and I will love him, and will manifest myself to him (John 14:21).

God is love. The word "manifest" means a number of different things: to speak, declare, or make known to humankind. In other words, because we have the Word and do the Word, God will show up when everything else is in disarray. When we keep His commandments, we are sowing to life and we will reap life, even in the midst of the storm.

As a result of this message that God had given me, our ministries have been praying for the church of the Lord Jesus Christ and our nation. We've been asking the Lord to forgive the church for its apathy, complacency, compromise, omissions, and secret sins. We've been asking God to forgive the church for withholding life, and for its failure to fulfill its call. We've been asking God to forgive America for its moral and spiritual decline, which has brought about the degrading of our culture—its carnality, impurity and impunity;

its greed and materialism; and its vanity and self-obsession. We have also been praying for the leadership of the church and our nation, because the Word clearly details the judgment that will come when leaders make a decision to force the nation of Israel to divide its land. God gave the land to Israel, and the Jewish people have a 3,900-year history with this land and a 3,000 year history with the city of Jerusalem.

A Tour of God's Promises to Abram

Let's explore Scripture and see what God's Word says about this matter. Look at what God said to Abram:

Now the Lord had said unto Abram, Get thee out of thy country, and from thy kindred, and from thy father's house, unto a land that I will shew thee: And I will make of thee a great nation, and I will bless thee, and make thy name great; and thou shalt be a blessing: And I will bless them that bless thee, and curse him that curseth thee: and in thee shall all families of the earth be blessed (Genesis 12:1-3).

God chose Israel, not because they were better than anyone else, but because He wanted a nation through which He could demonstrate to the world that if people do things His way, He will send blessings their way. They would demonstrate for the rest of the world that He is the true and living God.

As long as Israel walked in God's way, keeping the covenant that God had given them, blessings came their way. They became the strongest military power on earth, at the time. They also became the most prosperous nation. They became the envy of the world until they forgot about the Lord their God, kicked Him out of their public square, and began to worship other gods. They started planting seeds of death, disobeying God's written Word and His covenant. The end result was negative judgment, so much so that eventually, they were banished and dispersed all over the world.

Read what God continued to say to Abram, remembering that even the smallest part of the Word must come to pass.

And the LORD said unto Abram, after that Lot was separated from him, Lift up now thine eyes, and look from the place where thou art northward, and southward, and eastward, and westward: For all the land which thou seest, to thee will I give it, and to thy seed for ever. And I will make thy seed as the dust of the earth: so that if a man can number the dust of the earth, then shall thy seed also be numbered (Genesis 13:14-16).

Note this verse: *For all the land which thou seest, to thee will I give it, and to thy seed forever.* From Isaac and Jacob all the way to every Israeli today—this land would belong to them. God said, "forever," and He meant forever and ever, to every generation.

Arise, walk through the land in the length of it and in the breadth of it; for I will give it unto thee. Then Abram removed his tent, and came and dwelt in the plain of Mamre, which is in Hebron, and built there an altar unto the Lord (vv. 17-18).

Hebron is what is now called the West Bank in Israel. Abram dwelt in the West Bank and built an altar to the Lord.

A Tour of the Covenant

In the same day the Lord made a covenant with Abram, saying, Unto thy seed have I given this land, from the river of Egypt unto the great river, the river Euphrates: The Kenites, and the Kenizzites, and the Kadmonites, and the Hittites, and the Perizzites, and the Rephaims, and the Amorites, and the Canaanites, and the Girgashites, and the Jebusites (Genesis 15:18-21).

A covenant is a bond that cannot be broken or changed. When someone entered into a covenant in Old Testament times, both parties would draw blood from their fingers, hands, or wrists, and rub the cuts together to signify that this blood covenant went both ways. As long as one party kept the covenant, the members were blood brothers and would defend each other to the death. If one party broke the covenant, the other one had the right to kill that person and his family. Entering into a covenant was serious business back then! Today, people sign contracts (which are covenants) and then decide that they can't pay. This is called bankruptcy!

God entered into a blood covenant with Abram, giving him

first the land and then the boundaries from the river Egypt to the great river Euphrates. If you took a map and marked the lines, you would see that it looked like a larger footprint than the current state of Israel and extended farther east.

Let's take a walk through the Word and see how the covenant God made with Abram plays out. Then you will understand why God said what He did to the nation. When God tells us what's ahead, it's not that God's saying, "I'm going to get you now." No, God is saying that if we cross His Word and His way, His Word must still come to pass. The longer we have been planting, the greater our harvest will be. On the positive side, the more we plant faith and patience, the greater our harvest of faith and patience will be.

And we desire that every one of you do shew the same diligence to the full assurance of hope unto the end: That ye be not slothful, but followers of them who through faith and patience inherit the promises (Hebrews 6:11-12).

In other words, if we plucked some fruit before it was completely ripe, we may be able to eat it, but if we waited until it was fully mature, we would have a luscious, full-sized, ripened harvest of fruit. Time is the accelerant. **Waiting a while for your harvest only means that when you do receive it, the harvest will be greater than it would be if the time between planting and reaping were shorter.** This is true whether the harvest is positive or negative.

And when Abram was ninety years old and nine, the LORD appeared to Abram, and said unto him, I am the Almighty God; walk before me, and be thou perfect. And I will make my covenant between me and thee, and will multiply thee exceedingly. And Abram fell on his face: and God talked with him, saying, As for me, behold, my covenant is with thee, and thou shalt be a father of many nations. Neither shall thy name any more be called Abram, but thy name shall be Abraham; for a father of many nations have I made thee. And I will make thee exceeding fruitful, and I will make nations of thee, and kings shall come out of thee. And I will establish my covenant between me and thee and thy seed after thee in their generations for an everlasting covenant, to be a God unto thee, and to thy seed after thee. And I will give unto thee, and to thy seed after thee, the land wherein thou art a stranger, all the land of Canaan, for an everlasting possession; and I will be their God (Genesis 17:1-8).

This was an everlasting covenant for an everlasting possession—all the land of Canaan, an area larger than the current state of Israel. In other words, no changes in the covenant would be made. God would do His part, but the covenant would never be changed.

When we see truth revealed in Scripture, we can't say, "But I think..." No. The Bible is God's Word. Our thinking is just our thoughts. We can't say, "But what about..." No. The Bible is God speaking to us.

O ye seed of Israel his servant, ye children of Jacob, his chosen ones. He is the Lord our God; his judgments are in all the earth. Be ye mindful always of his covenant; the word which he commanded to a thousand generations; even of the covenant which he made with Abraham, and of his oath unto Isaac; and hath confirmed the same to Jacob for a law, and to Israel for an everlasting covenant, saying, Unto thee will I give the land of Canaan, the lot of your inheritance (1 Chronicles 16:13–18).

Read that passage through again. I don't know what part of these verses people don't understand. God made Himself very clear. Now, if you don't believe the Word is true, or if you hold the position that you can accept parts of the Bible you like and reject those you don't, that's between you and God. I am writing to born-again, blood-washed believers to whom the Bible is the final Word. I am writing to people who say, "If God said it, then I believe it; it's all settled." If you're not one of those, this teaching will not find a home with you. But I happen to be one of those who know that the Bible is God's Word. I know that it comes to pass, and I know that Jesus said that every man, woman, boy, and girl on the earth will be judged by one Book.

Here's what the Lord prophesied to Joel:

I will also gather all nations, and will bring them down into the valley of Jehoshaphat, and will plead with them there for my people and for my heritage Israel, whom they have scattered among the nations, and parted my land (Joel 3:2).

Armageddon will be in the valley of Jehoshaphat. The word "parted" means divided. If you study your Bible—especially the books of Ezekiel, Daniel, and Revelation—you know what's going to happen to the nations that have been forcing Israel to divide the land in the name of peace. This will result in their judgment in Armageddon.

Let's take a look at some other Scriptures. When I finish, you'll see why this is so critical to what's happening in our world today.

And in that day will I make Jerusalem a burdensome stone for all people: all that burden themselves with it shall be cut in pieces, though all the people of the earth be gathered together against it (Zechariah 12:3).

Jerusalem is a *burdensome stone* today. The entire world—the United Nations—is fighting about one city, Jerusalem and one nation, Israel. This will eventually be the reason for World War III. The entire world is turning against Israel. Only a few nations in the United Nations will abstain from opposing them, and even though the United States ostensibly is a supporter of Israel, in reality we aren't.

Let me show you why I make this statement: "*And it shall come to pass in that day, that I will seek to destroy all the nations that come against Jerusalem*" *(Zechariah 12:9)*. I am not going to attempt to reference all the Scriptures concerning this, because there are more than one hundred verses that support what I'm saying. Did God mean what He said? Yes, I think He did. And remember, not even the smallest part of His Word will fail to come to pass.

> *By little and little I will drive them out from before thee, until thou be increased, and inherit the land. And I will set thy bounds from the Red sea even unto the sea of the Philistines, and from the desert unto the river: for I will deliver the inhabitants of the land into your hand; and thou shalt drive them out before thee. Thou shalt make no covenant with them, nor with their gods. They shall not dwell in thy land, lest they make thee sin against me: for if thou serve their gods, it will surely be a snare unto thee (Exodus 23:30-33).*

Again, God is talking about the circumference of the land, which is larger than the current State of Israel. Notice God's warning against making a covenant with the inhabitants of the land. In other words, there should be no land deals for peace, because that would divide the land.

Chapter Seven

The Consequences of Violating the Covenant

Every world power that has either controlled or occupied the land of Israel has become a former world power, or has lost power like Great Britain did. America is now experiencing the consequences—or you could say the curses—of Middle East policies made by the last four U.S. presidents: two Republican and two Democrat. All four of these presidents have pressured Israel to divide its land for peace, and the current administration is doing so also. Yet, every nation that has done this has lost its place of power.

Both Democrats and Republicans have been opposed to God's Word and to the preservation of His covenant land ever since the Madrid Conference of October 1991. The United States' participation in Israel's destiny has been flawed when placed in this context of the Word of God. As a result, the United States has been experiencing the consequences. If America continues to support these "land for peace approaches," we can expect further lifting of the Lord's protective hand in greater measure.

Now, let me give you some exhibits since 1991, since the United States' policy changed under George H.W. Bush, showing you some of the events and the consequences.

- October 18, 1991: The United States announced the Madrid Peace Conference with Russia, Israel, other Arab nations and the Palestinians. Two days later, October 20th, 1991, the Oakland fire storm happened, the greatest fire and loss of life since 1906 in the United States, costing $2.5 billion.

- October 30 and November 1, 1991: The Madrid Middle East Peace Conference continued and on the same day a perfect storm, the worst storm in one hundred years, covered the United States' east coast, even damaging President Bush's home.

- August 24, 1992: Round six of the peace talks resumed in Washington, D.C. Israel came with an autonomy plan for the Palestinians. On the same day, Hurricane Andrew hit, the worst natural disaster in United States history to that time, and cost $27 billion.

- February 18-25, 1993: The new administration and the new United States Secretary of State Christopher visited Israel and seven Arab nations to restart this land for peace deal. On February 26, 1993, the first World Trade Center bombing happened. Six people were killed and more than a thousand were injured. There was $750 million worth of damage.

- March 10 and March 15-17, 1993: Secretary Christopher held a press conference on Israel and Israeli Prime

Minister Rabin met with President Clinton and others. At the same time, the Storm of the Century occurred, stretching from Central America to Canada and affecting almost 40 percent of the nation. More than 318 people died, and damages were $3-6 billion.

- April 27 through September, 1993: Israeli Palestinian negotiations continued in Oslo, Norway. Israel and the Palestine Liberation Organization signed a compromised agreement at the White House. From May to September 1993, the most devastating and widespread floods in modern U.S. history occurred in the Midwest. Thirty-eight people died, and the cost was more than $21 billion.

- January 16, 1994: President Clinton and Syrian President al-Assad made statements supporting the Oslo agreements as the first step to peace. The next day, January 17, the Norwich earthquake happened, the second most destructive natural disaster in U.S. history. (By the way, this was ground zero of the pornography industry in the US.) Damages were $15.3 billion.

- March 2, 1997: In response to Israel building housing units in east Jerusalem, the Palestine Liberation Organization chairman Yasser Arafat arrived in Washington, D.C. for a meeting he requested with President Clinton. They met the next day and issued public statements critical of Israel. The Mississippi and the Ohio valley flooded and there was a tornado outbreak with 67 people killed and incurring $1 billion in costs. President Clinton's home state of Arkansas was devastated by tornadoes.

- September 24, 1998: President Clinton said he would meet with Prime Minister Netanyahu and Yasser Arafat to pressure Israel to accept a plan to give up 13 percent of their land. From September 24-28, Hurricane George pounded the Gulf of Mexico with 110-mile per hour winds, heavy rains, and flooding, causing $5.9 billion in damages. It dissipated when Arafat left the United States.

- November 30, 1998: The second Middle East Donors Conference of the United States Department of State opened with 50 countries. They pledged $3 billion to the Palestinians, including President Clinton's pledge of an extra $400 million. On November 30 and December 1, the stock market had a massive selloff, with the Dow Jones falling 260 points. The European stock market experienced the third largest selloff in history. Billions of dollars were lost.

- August 25 through September 10, 2001: President George W. Bush, along with Secretary Powell and U.S. ambassador to Israel, Kurtzer, with Saudi corroboration, prepared the most comprehensive plan and message ever offered by a United States president for dividing Israel's land. The plan was nearly complete by September 10, and on September 11, terrorists used two airplanes to attack the World Trade Center towers in New York, one to attack the Pentagon in Washington, D.C., and one that was intended for either the White House or Congress that crashed in Pennsylvania. Nearly 3,000 people died, and there were more than $40 billion in damages.

- September 30, 2002: President Bush refused to move the United States Embassy from Tel Aviv to Israel, ignoring the sense of the United States Congress which it had expressed in its state department's spending bill. Two days later, Hurricane Lili became the first hurricane to hit land. From October 2-31, two snipers paralyzed Washington D.C.; the first shooting was within 24 hours of Bush's decision not to move the embassy.

- November 7, 2002: President Bush hosted a dinner at the beginning of Ramadan for Arab ambassadors. He honored Islam as the revelation of God's word in the holy Qur'an. From November 10-12, U.S. official David Satterfield flew to Israel to pressure Israel and Palestinian officials to complete the road map, another phrase of the land for peace deal. From November 9-11, 88 tornadoes slashed through seven states, one of the worst November tornado outbreaks in U.S. history.

- August 15. 2005: 63,000 Israeli soldiers and police delivered eviction notices to Israeli settlers living in Gaza and northern Samaria. On October 17, Israeli Prime Minister Ariel Sharon authorized mandatory evacuation of residents refusing to leave the Gaza. On August 22,

President Bush said, "My vision, my hope, is that one day we'll see two states—two democratic states—living side-by-side in peace." From October 23-29, Hurricane Katrina, the largest disaster in United States history, hit Louisiana, Mississippi, and Alabama, devastating New Orleans and forcing one million people from their homes. 225,000 homes were destroyed, 473,000 people were without work, and the estimated cost to insurers was $40.4 billion. The United States government spent up to $112 and $200 billion. The great financial collapse of 2008 during the last days of the Bush presidency is also attributed to this same thing.

I've given you a few examples of what happened when the U.S., along with other nations, participated in negotiating land for peace deals. I can identify 57 such events just up to 2005. Notice that the events get bigger and more costly in terms of loss of life, jobs, property, and money. Today, the United States government continues to follow those policies. The Lord says to tell the nation that judgment is coming again. Notice that judgment comes in different forms—weather, economic loss, terrorist attacks or other disasters.

What Can You Do?

Many people love to quote Second Chronicles 7:14, but it's important to look at that verse in context. Solomon had obeyed God, giving many tithes and offerings to the building of the temple.

He had finished the house of God.

And the Lord appeared to Solomon by night, and said unto him, I have heard thy prayer, and have chosen this place to myself for an house of sacrifice (2 Chronicles 7:12).

God then tells him what will happen in the future, if certain things occur: *"If I shut up heaven that there be no rain, or if I command the locusts to devour the land, or if I send pestilence among my people"* *(v. 13).*

Remember, 90% of the people in the world at that time farmed their own food and raised their own cattle, so if it didn't rain, they experienced unprecedented economic disaster. No rain meant no crops, which meant no money. There would be no work harvesting the crops and nothing with which to feed the animals.

If the locusts devoured the land, the crops would still be destroyed, bringing economic destruction. Pestilence, sickness, disease, and other disasters would also bring about extreme trials. God then says:

If my people, which are called by my name, shall humble themselves, and pray, and seek my face, and turn from their wicked ways; then will I hear from heaven, and will forgive their sin, and will heal their land (v. 14).

Do you see why the context is so important? In the midst of pending disaster, God says that if His people—and if you are a believer, you are a member of the body of Christ—humble themselves, pray, seek His face, and turn from wickedness, He will forgive their sin, and will heal their land.

Believer, God needs you! Wherever Jesus isn't manifest the way He should be, you are to fill all in all, in every place in the world. Look at Ephesians 1:22-23:

> *And hath put all things under his feet, and gave him to be the head over all things to the church, which is his body, the fulness of him that filleth all in all.*

We are that which fills all in all. We are a filler; we are supposed to supply an area that is not full already. Jesus has gone to heaven and is seated at the right hand of God. He's put up His feet, expecting His enemies to be made His footstool (see Hebrews 10:12-13). The church is tasked with keeping His enemies under His feet, but that cannot happen if His people don't do these things.

I want to identify some of the things that caused the nations of the world to get to where they are today. God has called me to several countries in Europe, places that have experienced the great revivals of the 16th through the 19th centuries. Although they experienced massive moves of God, today they are some of the least godly places on earth.

If we were to look at a map showing distribution of the world's major religions, we would see that the United States, most of Africa, and India are the places today with the most evangelical Christians. We think of the latter two as mission destinations, because we think in terms of economic poverty, not spiritual poverty which is actually worse than economic poverty. Spiritual wealth can handle natural poverty!

There are more Christians in China, a communist nation, than there are in Europe. In Europe, less than three percent of the population is born again. That is not the will of God! Look at what the Word says:

For this is good and acceptable in the sight of God our Saviour; who will have all men to be saved, and to come unto the knowledge of the truth (1 Timothy 2:3-4).

The only places that have as few Christians as Europe are northern Africa, Indonesia, and the Middle East—nations that follow Islam. If you were God and had designed the church to be filler where supply is lacking, wouldn't you send your people to these places? Why has this happened in nations that used to be primarily Christian nations? Let's take another look at Second Chronicles 7:14:

If my people, which are called by my name, shall humble themselves, and pray, and seek my face, and turn from their wicked ways; then will I hear from heaven, and will forgive their sin, and will heal their land.

Yes, there will be opposition to God's truth—these things will happen—but if God's people do the following things, then God has promised to forgive and heal.

- First, the body of Christ must humble themselves. When the church comes to the place that the Word of God is not the only standard by which it operates, when it gets secular education, public acceptance, and its own intellect and feelings involved in a matter, the church has lifted itself into a prideful position. To receive God's promise, the church has to bow down only to God and His Word.

- Second, they need to pray. If the church is not aware of its dependency, it's not praying a lot.

- Third, the church needs to seek God's face. Seeking God's face is not holding just church services; it's intentionally and regularly spending extended time before God in intercession.

- Fourth, God's people need to turn from their wicked ways.

Only when we do these four things, will we hear from heaven and receive God's forgiveness and healing. Much has happened in our country. There has been degradation in our culture, eliminating God from our schools and public square and accepting lifestyles that the Word of God opposes. I could go on and on. We've turned away from God, and that brings judgment. On top of all that, we are trying to force Israel to divide the land that God said was theirs forever. That is why the Lord has said, "Son and daughter, My mercy has been shown to you all this time. Turn. Stop. There's a brick wall ahead. You've hit it at 5 mph, 30 mph, and 70 mph, but now you've floored your accelerator, and you're about to hit it at 120 mph. If you do, the consequences are going to be disastrous!"

Yes, there's grace, but grace and judgment can reside in the same space. If we humble ourselves, pray and seek His face, and turn from any way that's opposite to God's way, let me tell you what our end result will be. We will have victory when death is all around us! God will show Himself to us. He'll warn us when we're in danger. He'll say, "Don't go to work today. Don't drive that route today." He'll tell us whatever is necessary to save our lives and the lives of our families.

God wants to manifest His love to you. You can declare victory over death! You can declare His manifested love (see Psalm 91). That's why you can shout!

Look at First John 1:

> *That which was from the beginning, which we have heard, which we have seen with our eyes, which we have looked upon, and our hands have handled, of the Word of life; (For the life was manifested, and we have seen it, and bear witness, and shew unto you that eternal life, which was with the Father, and was manifested unto us;) That which we have seen and heard declare we unto you, that ye also may have fellowship with us: and truly our fellowship is with the Father, and with his Son Jesus Christ (vv.1-3).*

The life he's talking about is that of Jesus. He was shown to us. We have seen and heard. We can have fellowship with the Father and His Son. The word "fellowship" in the Greek is *koinonia*, which means a partnership. We are partners with the Father and His Son, Jesus Christ.

"And these things write we unto you, that your joy may be full" *(v. 4).* When our joy is full, we don't have room for any more, because we're so blessed!

"This then is the message which we have heard of him, and declare unto you, that God is light, and in him is no darkness at all. If we say that we have fellowship with him, and walk in darkness, we lie, and do not the truth" (vv. 5-6). We walk in darkness by going against the Word.

"But if we walk in the light, as he is in the light, we have fellowship one with another, and the blood of Jesus Christ his Son cleanseth us from all sin" (v. 7). The blood cleanses us only if we are walking in the light. Have you always walked in the light? Have you walked in darkness, even though you've been saved? John is not done yet.

If we say that we have no sin, we deceive ourselves, and the truth is not in us. If we confess our sins, he is faithful and just to forgive us our sins, and to cleanse us from all unrighteousness (vv. 8-9).

If we confess—or acknowledge—our sins, He is trustworthy and sure and just. He is the judge to forgive us, to lay aside our sin.

My little children, these things write I unto you, that ye sin not. And if any man sin, we have an advocate with the Father, Jesus Christ the righteous: And he is the propitiation

for our sins: and not for ours only, but also for the sins of the
whole world. And hereby we do know that we know him, if
we keep his commandments. He that saith, I know him, and
keepeth not his commandments, is a liar, and the truth is not
in him (1 John 2:1-4).

John is talking to the church. He's saying, "Don't sin, but if you do, you have an advocate, *parakletos* in the Greek—a counselor, a lawyer—who advocates with the Father not only on your behalf, but also on behalf of everyone in the world."

Clearly, grace does not mean that we no longer have to confess our sins. In order for a church to be a grace-only body, significant chunks of the Bible would have to be deleted, including all of First John 1 and 2. Make a commitment to rightly divide the truth— to live knowing that not only does all grace abound toward you, but also that you will reap what you sow. Furthermore, make a commitment to support the Biblical position on issues, including the truth that God has given the land to Israel. Don't risk putting yourself or your family into a position whereby you and they will reap the consequences of not following the instructions in the Word of God wholeheartedly.

Chapter Eight

Grace in the Midst of Problems

In the previous chapters, we explored what happens when people do not have a solid understanding of the issue of grace vs. judgment, based on solid Biblical teaching. We have taken an extensive tour of Scriptures on these subjects, looking at the different definitions of the words and exploring the context so we can stand firm when the waves of controversy about this issue sweep the country.

In this chapter, let's explore another problem—the immature understanding of what happens when a person is walking in faith and experiences problems. As I have said, I have been in the ministry more than forty years, and I grew up during a move of the Holy Spirit. This was a time when most ministers did not teach the Bible, they only took one or two Scriptures and preached from those verses. People rarely brought their Bibles to church. Once the preacher started ministering, the Bible was closed and people were moved by the oratorical skill of the minister—his or her ability to put words together that sounded good and titillated the ears of the people in their congregation.

When I was a boy, the only time people were taught was in

Sunday school. Although God restored the office of teacher to the body of Christ, at the time when I started my ministry, many of the students of the original faith teachers began to teach things beyond what the original teachers had taught, giving rise to much confusion. Many ministers wanted to put their imprimatur on the teaching, saying, "I didn't get this from somebody else; it is my own." But when it comes to God's Word, there is nothing new! God's Word is never about a person appearing to be highly educated or highly anointed; it is never about the amount of revelation a person has received. God's Word is not about us! Teaching is only about dispensing God's Word.

As a result of this teaching, people began to get the belief that nothing ever goes wrong if a person is operating in faith; hard times won't come his or her way. When anyone began to have a hard time, many in the body of Christ would take the view that the favor of God did not rest on that person anymore. They even ascribed positions that clearly represent an immature understanding of faith, to the point of blaming the person undergoing the hardship.

Jesus never participated in the blame game! Let's look at Scripture to understand where tests and trials come from. The only reason people undergo assault is because Satan is trying to make a victim of them. When you ascribe their loss of favor to God or their lack of faith to some other reason, you only add more problems to the person being assaulted.

As we've already seen, grace is not our position in Christ. It is not what we do when we sin, or what we don't do when we sin. Grace is the manifested measure of the Holy Spirit bringing about the fruit and gifts of the Holy Spirit as Paul tells us in 2 Corinthians 12:9: "*And he said unto me, My grace is sufficient for thee: for my strength is made perfect in weakness. Most gladly therefore will I rather glory in my infirmities, that the power of Christ may rest upon me.*" Paul goes on to say: "*Therefore I take pleasure in infirmities, in reproaches, in necessities, in persecutions, in distresses for Christ's sake: for when I am weak, then am I strong" (v. 10).*

For the Anointing

Notice the phrase: *for Christ's sake.* In most cases, if we were to say, "For his sake," that would mean that we were doing something for that person. In this context, however, the phrase doesn't mean that at all. First, we have to look at the word "Christ." Christ is not Jesus' last name. The word "Christ" is *Christos* in the Greek, and it means the anointed one. It refers particularly to the Messiah—Jesus.

Jesus was anointed when John baptized Him in the Jordan River and the Holy Spirit descended upon Him like a dove (see Matthew 3:16). Notice the phrase *like a dove.* The Word says in John 1 that Jesus was full of grace. This word "full" means that grace was over Him or it came upon Him.

Scripture tells us more about that fullness of grace in Acts 10:38: "*How God anointed Jesus of Nazareth with the Holy Ghost and with power: who went about doing good, and healing all that were oppressed of the devil; for God was with him.*" Jesus was anointed *with* something. To be anointed means to be poured over or smeared with. Jesus was anointed with the Holy Ghost and with power. God was with Jesus by the Holy Ghost on Him, empowering Him to do all the things that He did on the face of the earth. Notice that Jesus didn't do any miracles until He was baptized in the Jordan River.

In this context, *for Christ's sake* means "for the anointing." The word "sake" in the Greek is *huper*, a word that means "over." Whatever Paul says here is *"for the anointing."*

Look at verse 9 again: *"And he said unto me, My grace is sufficient for thee: for my strength is made perfect in weakness."* God says that His grace is His strength. The Greek word for strength is *dunamis*, which is a miracle working ability. The Lord says, *"My strength is made perfect in weakness."* The word "perfect" means to complete; therefore, He's saying, "My strength completes you. Your weakness can't get the job done, but My strength, or My supernatural ability, will get it done for you."

Paul got revelation of this when he said, *most gladly would he rather glory in his infirmities, reproaches and necessities, that the power of Christ may rest upon him.* The word "power" is *dunamis*. Once again, we see that grace is the power of the Holy Spirit, the strength of the Holy Spirit, the assistance of the Holy Spirit, and the manifested measure of the Holy Spirit, which brings about the results of God and the work of God.

God Does Not Cause Your Problems

Let's look at an example of a problem and Jesus' response to it: *"And as Jesus passed by, he saw a man which was blind from his birth. And his disciples asked him, saying, Master, who did sin, this man, or his parents, that he was born blind?" (John 9:1-2).* Jesus and His disciples pass a person who is blind, and they immediately ask the question that human beings typically ask—*Who is at fault?* In other words, here is a problem, so who is to blame?

Now, there are times when we produce our own unique set of circumstances because of bad decisions we make. There is no denying that. Life is a series of choices, and we all make them—good and bad. We have all made some wonderful decisions, and we have also made some horrific decisions that we would take back in a second if we could. But that is the way that life works. We just have to keep on going!

Let's see if Jesus will play the blame game with them. *"Jesus answered, Neither hath this man sinned, nor his parents" (v. 3).* Jesus answers the question and then continues. (Remember, the New Testament was not written with punctuation marks, so they were added by man.) What did Jesus mean when He said, *"but that the works of God should be made manifest in him" (v. 3)?* He wasn't saying that before this man was born, God decided that He was going to make him blind so Jesus could come along one day and give him back his sight, and He would receive the glory. We would call that abuse. It would be as if I had thrown one of my children down the stairs headfirst, injuring him severely, just so I could lay hands on him so he could get healed. Nobody would say that my act was a righteous one!

But that's what people say about God all the time. They say God did this or that so He could get the glory. No! Jesus wasn't playing the blame game. He was giving an answer to the problem.

Here's another example of this:

Now a certain man was sick, named Lazarus, of Bethany, the town of Mary and her sister Martha. (It was that Mary which anointed the Lord with ointment, and wiped his feet with her hair, whose brother Lazarus was sick.) Therefore his sisters sent unto him, saying, Lord, behold, he whom thou lovest is sick (John 11:1-3).

Lazarus was sick, but Jesus didn't get into the blame game of why this must have happened. He didn't say, "This must be because he didn't have the anointing." When Jesus heard about it, He simply said, *"This sickness is not unto death, but for the glory of God, that the Son of God might be glorified thereby"* (v. 4).

God didn't make the man sick so Jesus could come and heal him. Rather than play the blame game, Jesus announced what was going to happen. He declared, "God is going to receive glory when I get there."

Faith Can Exist in the Middle of Your Problem

An immature understanding of how living by faith works is to assume that faith is not being exercised if there is a problem. I want to show you from the Word of God that this is not true. In Philippians 4, the apostle Paul says: *"Not that I speak in respect of want: for I have learned, in whatsoever state I am, therewith to be content" (v. 11).* Paul wouldn't have said, *"in whatsoever state I am"* if the only state he was ever in was blessed, prosperous, and healthy.

In other words, Paul says, "I have learned what my mental attitude should be, regardless of what has come my way."

He goes on to say: "*I know both how to be abased, and I know how to abound: every where and in all things I am instructed both to be full and to be hungry, both to abound and to suffer need" (v. 12).* The phrase "how to be abased," *tapeinoo,* means, "I know how to be humiliated, if necessary. I know how to bring myself low. I know how to be humble."The phrase 'how to abound," *perisseuo,* means, "I know how to have abundance. I know how to have increase."

When Paul says, "*every where and in all things I am instructed both to be full and to be hungry, both to abound and to suffer need,"* he's not saying, "I get out of faith, so I suffer need, and I am in faith, so I abound." No.

The next verse says, "*I can do all things through Christ which strengtheneth me" (v. 13).* The word "do" in the Greek is *ischuo,* which means, "I know how to exercise force. I know how to prevail against whatsoever comes my way." Thus, Paul is saying, "I can exercise force in whatever comes my way through Christ—the anointing, the power, the Holy Ghost—which strengthens me." The word "strengthen," *endunamoo,* means to empower. The anointing, or the Holy Spirit, will empower Paul.

Again, an immature reading of faith says that you are out of faith if you have any challenges, but Paul is saying, "I have learned what attitude to take when times are bad and when times are good; when my coffers are full, and when my checkbook is empty; when my body feels good, and when I can't get out of bed."Why? Because he knows that through Christ, he has power to deal with it.

Paul's Experience with Problems

Let's take a look at some of Paul's experiences. But before we do this, let's look at Paul's source of insight found in 2 Corinthians 12:1: "*It is not expedient for me doubtless to glory. I will come to visions and revelations of the Lord.*" In other words, the Lord would appear to Paul and teach him. The Lord would give Paul revelations, understanding in the realm of the spirit that he didn't get through natural learning. The Lord would give him revelations of the kingdom of God—how God operates, how Satan operates, what the Word of God does, and what to do with the Word of God.

And lest I should be exalted above measure through the abundance of the revelations, there was given to me a thorn in the flesh, the messenger of Satan to buffet me, lest I should be exalted above measure (v. 7).

The phrase *above measure* refers to the measure of visions and revelations that Paul was walking in. The thorn in the flesh is referred to as the messenger of Satan. The word "messenger," *angelous* in the Greek, is found 188 times in the New Testament and 181 of those times, this word is translated as angel. Seven times—as in this verse—*angelous* is translated as messenger, and in this context, it refers to a demon spirit sent from Satan. This demon spirit's assignment was to come against Paul, to buffet him, which means to strike repeatedly, to slap again and again, lest Paul should be exalted above measure.

Second Corinthians 11 tells us some of the things that Paul, this great man of faith, experienced that caused him to say: "I know how to be abased and how to abound."

Are they ministers of Christ? (I speak as a fool) I am more; in labours more abundant, in stripes above measure, in prisons more frequent, in deaths oft. Of the Jews five times received I forty stripes save one. Thrice was I beaten with rods, once was I stoned, thrice I suffered shipwreck, a night and a day I have been in the deep; in journeyings often, in perils of waters, in perils of robbers, in perils by mine own countrymen, in perils by the heathen, in perils in the city, in perils in the wilderness, in perils in the sea, in perils among false brethren; in weariness and painfulness, in watchings often, in hunger and thirst, in fastings often, in cold and nakedness. Beside those things that are without, that which cometh upon me daily, the care of all the churches (vv. 23-28).

The word "care," *merimna*, means a distraction. Bishops, those assigned to oversee churches, understand what Paul is talking about when he identifies the daily care of all the churches as a heavy responsibility. Paul says that he was tied to a pole and beaten with thirty-nine lashes, five different times. If you want a vivid visual picture of this, watch *Twelve Years a Slave*, a recent movie about a free slave in the North who was kidnapped and taken to the South. The hands of this disobedient slave were tied to a whipping post, and he was stripped. He was then whipped with a lash that not only caused great pain, but also lacerated his flesh. Paul was tied and whipped like this five times.

Paul goes on to say, "Three times, I was beaten with a rod, and once, I was stoned." Death by stoning is one of the most violent ways a person can die. The people who stoned Paul left him for dead, and his disciples stood around him. Then he stood on his feet! Power was available to Paul!

There's more. Three times, Paul was shipwrecked, and countless times this man of faith was put in prison. You can read about one of those imprisonments in Acts 16. Paul and Silas were brought before the judge for casting Satan out of a demon-possessed girl. The judge decreed that they were to be stripped and beaten.

And when they had laid many stripes upon them, they cast them into prison, charging the jailor to keep them safely: Who, having received such a charge, thrust them into the inner prison [dungeon], and made their feet fast in the stocks (v. 23-24, emphasis mine).

My wife and I recently went to the Coliseum in Rome, a place where gladiator fights were held and Christians were killed by lions or other animals. The Coliseum was large enough for an NFL football game, seating 60,000 or 70,000 people. Across the square from the Coliseum was a place where the Christians or the gladiators were jailed, and on the other side of that was the place where Paul and Silas—and later, Peter—were imprisoned.

We went in that underground prison that was built out of

nothing but stone. The post where the chains were hooked is still there. There's no bathroom. There are no lights. There's no air-conditioning. There is nothing but darkness and coldness.

Everything Happens for a Reason

Why does Satan assign a demon spirit to this man? How does Paul respond? In order to answer these questions, I need to give you some background. As we've seen from Scripture, just because you might have any kind of attack, including a financial problem, a health problem, a family problem, or any other kind of issue, this does not necessarily mean that the favor of God is no longer on you. It doesn't necessarily mean that you are not operating in faith.

Everything happens for a reason, and the reason can be found in the parable of the sower in Mark 4. *"The sower soweth the word"* *(v. 14)*. God called Paul to minister the Word to the Gentiles. His job was to sow, or plant, the Word. God had selected him for this purpose, and that is what he did. He traveled all over the known world, taking the Gospel with him. God is the ultimate sower, but God uses men to do it through the foolishness of preaching. Paul is a carrier of the Word; he is a spreader of the message.

> *And these are they by the way side, where the word is sown;*
> *but when they have heard, Satan cometh immediately, and*
> *taketh away the word that was sown in their hearts. And*
> *these are they likewise which are sown on stony ground; who,*
> *when they have heard the word, immediately receive it with*
> *gladness; and have no root in themselves, and so endure but*

*for a time: afterward, when affliction or persecution ariseth for
the word's sake, immediately they are offended (vv. 15-17).*

Persecution occurs when pressure is brought against you by
people. The word "offended" is *skandalizo,* and its purpose is to
make you quit, give up, fall into sin, or stop. Satan used persecution
against Paul. Being beaten and stoned was persecution. Hunger was
affliction. In other words, Satan assigned a demon spirit to raise
up people to persecute Paul, and if he couldn't use people, he used
circumstances to afflict him. Why? So he could stop all of that
abundance of revelation that God had given Paul. He wanted to
make him quit, give up, back down, and become offended and angry
with God. Paul was sowing the Word—doing what He was called
to do—when this affliction and persecution happened.

At times, some people say, "Lord, I am doing what You told me
to do. You told me to tithe, and I'm doing it. You told me to preach,
and I'm doing it. Why, then, are You allowing this to happen to me?"

It is not God's job to intervene yet. You have a job to do before He gets to do His.

When affliction and persecution occur, you are immediately
tempted to say, "Where did I miss it?" However, you must understand
that this may not necessarily be the case. There are times that you
do miss it, but you may not have missed it at all this time. You may
be doing exactly what you are supposed to be doing, and affliction
and persecution are coming your way precisely because of that.
Sickness and disease may be attacking you because you are obeying

God. The enemy may be coming against you, precisely because of what you have done in obedience to God.

Word-Based Thinking

You need to get your thinking straight. Much of the faith teaching, when I first came into the ministry, was what I call the "lollipop" kind. God was like Santa Claus, and all you had to do was say certain things and do certain things, and you would receive money or whatever you needed with no trouble and no problem.

Let me tell you what happens when people follow that kind of teaching. When they don't get results, they become discouraged, because Satan will immediately hit them with affliction and persecution for that Word. They then are at risk of becoming offended. They may even stop going to church altogether. There are a lot of people like this today. They feel as if they were taken advantage of and lied to, although that wasn't necessarily the case. They just received bad teaching. There's more to living a life of faith than following teaching that says, "You don't have to do anything. All you have to do is believe."

Here's an analogy that's easy to understand. If someone asks me to pray that they get top grades in school, and I pray, it won't accomplish anything if that person doesn't study. There's no way that prayers for an excellent grade will be answered, if the student doesn't do his part.

Likewise, you have a part to play. When you can't do what you are supposed to do anymore—when you are at the end—that's where the anointing can pick up and take you past what you are capable of doing yourself and put you in a position of victory.

Chapter Nine

God's Amazing, All-Sufficient Grace

We have looked at the attacks Paul faced, and the truths from Scripture that a life of faith does not mean that affliction and persecutions won't come. It does mean, however, that there are certain things you must do before God's power and anointing will step in. What do you do when you face any of these tough attacks by Satan? Simply stated, you trust God. Here are the steps you need to take.

Why Is the Attack Happening?

You need to recognize why the attack is happening. Satan will not only use affliction and persecution, but he will also use the cares of this world, the deceitfulness of riches—either with you or against you—and the lust of other things to choke the Word and make it become unfruitful (see Mark 4). You have to remember that the attack may be happening because you are doing what God told you to be doing. You are sowing the Word. You are witnessing. You are performing for God as Paul was. In all of this, you refuse to be trapped and tripped up. You refuse to stumble or be enticed to sin.

If you do stumble and if you do sin, however, don't beat yourself up. First John 1:9 comes into play: "*If we confess [acknowledge] our sins, he is faithful and just to forgive us our sins, and to cleanse us from all unrighteousness" (emphasis mine).* As we've seen, John was talking to Christians (see First John 2:1). If you confess your sins, right standing with God will be restored. Nothing will be in your way to keep His assistance from reaching you.

Forgiveness is not automatic! If it was automatic, why did Paul tell us to come boldly to the throne of grace to receive mercy? Why did Paul tell us to confess our sins? Never trust the word of a preacher if that person can't show you teaching from the Word of God. We are under no obligation to accept teaching that is not Word-based.

Go to God

We must realize that God is not the source of our problem; we must acknowledge that He is the source of our answer: "*Let no man say when he is tempted [tested or tried], I am tempted of God: for God cannot be tempted with evil, neither tempteth he any man: But every man is tempted, when he is drawn away of his own lust, and enticed"* (*James 1:13-14, emphasis mine).* This echoes what Jesus says in Mark 4. In other words, the source of our answer is His grace, the manifestation of the Holy Spirit's power.

Stay in Faith

In the face of tough attacks, we can become offended. We can stumble. We must decide to stay in faith, however. We will stay in faith by seeking God for the word He wants us to announce. Don't say whatever comes to your mind in the middle of your situation. Get before God in prayer and say, "Holy Spirit, give me what You want me to say in the face of this issue. What do You want me to release out of my mouth?" He will give you a *rhema* word, a spoken word from God. Then you can speak in the midst of that situation and release God's Word out of your mouth into the midst of the problem.

Decide to believe the Word of God and receive what it says. If you're looking at the doctor's report that says you have an incurable disease, choose to believe God's Word that says you are healed. If you are looking at an empty bank account, choose to believe the Word of God that says that God will supply all your need. You are the one who decides whether you will receive what God's Word says or not.

Count It All Joy

In James 1:1, the twelve tribes are running all over the known world to avoid persecution. But look at what James says: "*My brethren, count it all joy when ye fall into divers temptations; "Knowing this, that the trying of your faith worketh patience. But let patience have her perfect work, that ye may be perfect and entire, wanting nothing*" (*vv. 2-4*).

In other words, we need to know how to be abased and how to abound. We need to know how to keep the right attitude, and not lose it. We need to keep ourselves together. The worst thing we can do is panic and start saying the wrong thing, doing the wrong thing, thinking the wrong thing, and acting the wrong way, because then we will give the devil a signed blank check to finish the job he has begun.

You may be experiencing pressure in your body, your finances, or in a life situation. If so, I'm here to tell you that it's not over! I've been in the fight a long time, and I can testify that it's not over unless you decide to say that it's over. Instead, choose to say, "I'm not going to be moved by what I see! I'm not going to be moved by what I feel! I'm only going to be moved by what I believe, and I believe God's Word! I count this situation as *all joy!*"

I realize, of course, this is easier said than done. Remember, you can do all things through the anointing, and the anointing is activated by your decision. If you believe and receive this teaching from God's Word, it will last you the rest of your life. It will get you through anything you will ever face. It will help you when the enemy wants to take you out!

The anointing will enable you to live in the fullness of your days. It will keep you from being sick in your body because of worry. It will keep you from financial ruin when you continue to make bad decisions. It will cause you to stop going to the wrong person for advice, which will only further mess up your life. It will cause you to go to God Almighty to get wisdom.

Paul's Response to Trials

And lest I should be exalted above measure through the abundance of the revelations, there was given to me a thorn in the flesh, the messenger of Satan to buffet me, lest I should be exalted above measure. For this thing I besought the Lord thrice, that it might depart from me (2 Corinthians 12:7-8).

Three times, Paul went to God and said, "God, will You stop this thing from messing with me? Stop the stonings and shipwrecks!" In other words, He said, "I understand, Lord, that this is a demon spirit." He didn't say, "Stop the people from doing this to me."

Your enemy is not flesh and blood. Your mother-in-law is not your enemy. Your father-in-law is not your enemy. There is a demon behind these folks, and this demon is using them against you. There is no sense in treating the symptom—go right to the source! Stop getting mad at the symptom and get angry at the source. Recognize that Satan is the source of your problem, and decide to deal with him instead of dealing with people. Walk in love with them and use your authority against Satan.

When Paul prayed, notice that the Lord did not answer him the first time. No doubt Satan whispered, "You're doing work for God; you have suffered all these things, and now God won't even answer you. Where is your God?"

Paul asked a second time, and God still did not answer him. Some of you say, "I have been seeking the Lord for a while now, and I can't seem to get an answer." God isn't in a hurry. You are the one in a hurry. He is not bound by time. He understands that if you do what you are supposed to do, everything will work out.

But Paul was still growing up. Paul was still learning. He was a human like us. So he asked the Lord a third time, and finally the Lord answered him and said, *"And he said unto me, My grace is sufficient for thee: for my strength is made perfect in weakness" (v. 9a).*

God told Paul, "My power, My anointing, and My miraculous ability is enough for you! My supernatural power is made complete in your inability." In other words, God said, "Son, I know you can't deal with that demon spirit. You couldn't beat a baby demon with one hand tied behind its back. But you don't have to take him down. Your Big Brother has already done that!" These are shouting words! Jesus has already defeated Satan!

Paul got it! The light came on. He received the revelation! *"Most gladly therefore will I rather glory* [brag] *in my infirmities* [my weaknesses, my inabilities, my failure to get the job done by myself], *that the* [supernatural] *power of Christ may rest upon me. Therefore I take pleasure in infirmities, in reproaches, in necessities, in persecutions, in distresses for Christ's sake: for when I am weak, then am I strong" (v. 9-10, emphasis mine).*

Notice Paul's attitude change: *Therefore I take pleasure.* Instead of saying, "Lord, why are You letting this happen to me," he is now saying, "I get it!" I take pleasure:

- In *infirmities*, a word meaning weaknesses and inabilities.

- In *reproaches*, when other people talk badly about him, causing him to become an individual whom people scorn.

- In *necessities*, a word that means dealing with lack or need, including financial problems.

- In *persecution*, which is pressure brought upon a person by Satan, who uses other people to bring it.

- In *distresses*, a word meaning calamity.

Again, do all of these things mean that Paul is out of favor with God? No! At least Paul sought the Lord for advice, instead of his friends. Stop talking to folks and start talking to God. Stop asking people for their opinion; consult the Holy Ghost. One word from God can change your attitude. One word from God can change your life forever. One word from God can change your life and release the power of God in your life.

Say, "I am taking pleasure in my weaknesses and inabilities. I take pleasure in people talking about me. I take pleasure in the fact that I have no money today. I take pleasure with these folks messing with me." The anointing was over Paul: *for when I am weak, then am I strong.* You need to keep your attitude, get back in faith, seek God for the Word to announce, decide to believe it and receive it, and count it all joy!

Turn Up the Praise

Let's return to Paul and Silas in the dungeon in Acts 16 and see how they responded. After Paul and Silas were stripped, beaten, thrown into prison, and chained to a post, they sang, "The joy of the Lord is my strength." It didn't matter what the dungeon smelled like. It didn't matter what it looked like. It didn't matter what was going on. They chose to believe the word God gave them, and the power of God showed up. The jail shook with an earthquake, and everybody's bands were loosed.

You'll see the power when you use the joy. When you praise, you will release the power, God's ability to move. If you give credit to God instead of to the circumstances, there will be a whole lot of shaking going on in your life! There is some shaking that is going to happen to your money. There is some shaking that is going to happen to your body. There is some shaking that is going to happen to your family. If you will do what God says to do, the power of God will be on its way!

Get ready to receive the manifestation of the power of God. Get ready to have your circumstances turned around. Get ready for the devil to be kicked out of your life. James saw tests and trials as an opportunity to get better, and that was Paul's attitude as well. You can see the circumstances as reason to doubt God, or you can see them as an opportunity to learn and grow. God's not using the tests and trials. Your trials don't come only to make you strong. They come to knock you out! But you can choose to say, "I know where this comes from, I know why it is here, and I know what to do about it."

Live in Patience

Look at James' advice: *"But let patience have her perfect work, that ye may be perfect and entire, wanting nothing" (James 1:4).* The trying of our faith works patience, but let patience run its course.

Too many people don't want to hear about patience, but sometimes we have to be patient in an unfair situation. It wasn't fair for Joshua and Caleb to be refused entrance to the Promised Land. They spoke the Word of God, yet they had to go in the wilderness for forty years with everybody else, even though they were right.

Understand this. Life is not fair. Life is not about comparing our lives to someone else's; it's about what we do with what we have, wherever we started. With the power of God, we can get anywhere. The power of God will knock out all the jealousy, all the envy, and all the covetousness.

God is just. At the end of the forty years, when that unbelieving generation died, Caleb said to Joshua, "I was forty years old when that happened, and now I am eighty. But I remember the word that God gave Moses concerning me. The power of God is upon me, so give me my mountain!"

The power of God can make up the difference! The date on our birth certificate may say that we are old, but the power of God can make us young! The power of God can keep us. The power of God can restore us. The power of God can deliver us. The power of God enabled Caleb and Joshua to enter the land and take the inhabitants. And their families got all of their inheritance.

One of the names of God is "the One who will make things right." We need to have enough patience to let Him work. Faith and patience enabled Abraham to inherit the promise, and the same will be true for us.

The reason we may have to wait is because God has to deal with other people, and it may take time for them to obey. For example, in the matter of giving, Luke 6:38 says, "*Give, and it shall be given unto you; good measure, pressed down, and shaken together, and running over, shall men give into your bosom. For with the same measure that ye mete withal it shall be measured to you again.*" If God wants to accomplish this through a person who chooses to disobey, we may have to wait. God will give a person space to come to his senses, but the day will come when that person will need somebody to step up for him, and he will have to wait as long as he made somebody else wait.

There may come a time, however, when the Lord will speak to someone else in order to accomplish His Word. If that person obeys, know that God will give us our return on sowing with interest! He always gives more!

If you need wisdom to know how to act, ask God for revelation. You don't need to see a psychiatrist. You don't need to buy a self-help book on how to handle stress. You don't need a girlfriend or boyfriend to help you through your situation. If you start acting and talking in unbelief, you will stop God's actions: "*But without faith it is impossible to please him: for he that cometh to God must believe that he is, and that he is a rewarder of them that diligently seek him*" (*Hebrews 11:6*).

Stay the course! Maybe the Lord has been working on you and you finally turned and started heading in the right direction. Satan can see that you have to take only two more steps before you get there, and that is when he will turn up the power. He doesn't want you to get blessed. Turn up the praise in the darkest hours just before dawn. That is the time to shout, because the God who makes things right, will make your situation right if you continue to walk in faith. His grace will be sufficient!

PRAYER OF SALVATION

God loves you—no matter who you are, no matter what your past. God loves you so much that He gave His one and only begotten Son for you. The Bible tells us that "...whoever believes in Him shall not perish but have eternal life" (John 3:16 NIV). Jesus laid down His life and rose again so that we could spend eternity with Him in heaven and experience His absolute best on earth. If you would like to receive Jesus into your life, say the following prayer out loud and mean it from your heart.

Heavenly Father, I come to You admitting that I am a sinner. Right now, I choose to turn away from sin, and I ask You to cleanse me of all unrighteousness. I believe that Your Son, Jesus, died on the cross to take away my sins. I also believe that He rose again from the dead so that I might be forgiven of my sins and made righteous through faith in Him. I call upon the name of Jesus Christ to be the Savior and Lord of my life. Jesus, I choose to follow You and ask that You fill me with the power of the Holy Spirit. I declare that right now I am a child of God. I am free from sin and full of the righteousness of God. I am saved in Jesus' name. Amen.

If you prayed this prayer to receive Jesus Christ as your Savior for the first time, please contact us on the Web at **www.harrisonhouse.com** to receive a free book.

Or you may write to us at

Harrison House • P.O. Box 35035 • Tulsa, Oklahoma 74153

The Harrison House Vision

Proclaiming the truth and the power

Of the Gospel of Jesus Christ

With excellence;

Challenging Christians to

Live victoriously,

Grow spiritually,

Know God intimately.